To my wife, Shternie.
You are a beacon of light, strength, wisdom,
and love.

LETTERS OF LIGHT

Rabbi Aaron L. Raskin

Sichos In English

Letters of Light

Published and Copyrighted by

Rabbi Aaron L. Raskin
287 Hicks Street
Brooklyn, N.Y. 11201
718-596-0069

Sichos In English
788 Eastern Parkway
Brooklyn, N.Y. 11213
718-778-5436
www.sichosinenglish.org

ISBN 1-8814-0074-3

TABLE OF CONTENTS

6

INTRODUCTION

There are an estimated 3,000 languages (not counting dialects) and more than 66,000 letters which make up the alphabets for these languages. Only one language and one alphabet is Divinely created, the letters having been formed and shaped by G-d alone. That language is *Lashon HaKodesh*, biblical Hebrew.

It is no wonder, then, that the Hebrew letters are multifaceted. The letters of the Hebrew alphabet, the *alef-beis*, are so rich with meaning that even Judaism's greatest scholars had to engage in lengthy study to understand why G-d made them as He did. Traditionally, Hebrew letters possess:

1) *Design*—the specific way each letter is formed. This form represents the Divine energy within each letter.

2) *Gematria*—each of the letters of the *alef-beis* represents a certain number, e.g., *alef* = 1, *beis* = 2, etc.

3) *Meaning*—each letter has many meanings, e.g., the letter *alef* stands for chief, to learn, wondrous, and much more. *Beis* means house, etc.

4) *Nekudos* (*vowels*)—most letters have a vowel that tells us how it is to be pronounced.

5) *Crowns*—some letters in the Torah have crowns—little lines drawn on the top of Hebrew letters—which add strength to the letters, e.g. גּ. Rabbi Akiva was famous for his expositions upon them. The crowns have their own special meanings beyond the scope of this work.

6) *Cantillation*—each word in the Torah has a musical note.

In this book we will deal with the first four topics. The rest we will leave for another time and another book.

For grammatical reasons, certain Hebrew letters have two different pronunciations (e.g., *beis* and *veis*, *kaf* and *chaf*, *pei* and *fei*, *shin* and *sin*, *tav* and *sav*) as you will find throughout this book. Regardless of its pronunciation in a particular word,

8

we will call the letter by its principal name (e.g., *beis, kaf, pei,* etc.)

It is important to note that many words in Hebrew, as in all Semitic languages,—though they sound phonetically different— share the same root and therefore are interrelated. For example, *alef, aluf* and *ulfana* all share the same common root of א = *alef,* ל = *lamed* and ף = *pei,* and so their meanings are connected.

Also, according to *Kabbalah,* when the same letters are transposed to form different words, they retain the common energy of their shared *gematria.* Because of this, the words maintain a connection in the different forms. We find a classic example of this with the words הצר, *hatzar* (troubles), רצה, *ratzah* (a desire to run passionately into the "ark" of Torah and prayer) and צהר, *tzohar* (a light that shines from within). All three words share the same three letters: *tzaddik, reish* and *hei* in different combinations. The Baal Shem Tov[1] explains[2] the connection between the words as follows: When one is experiencing troubles (*hatzar*), and one runs to study Torah and pray with great desire (*ratzah*), one is illuminated with a G-dly light from within (*tzohar*) that helps him transform his troubles into blessings.[3]

Because a Hebrew letter radiates light, insight and clarity, it is called an אות (*os*), connected to the passage[4] אתא בוקר (*asa boker*—"morning will come"). As such, we have chosen to call our book *Letters of Light*—the light of wisdom and understanding which emanates from the letters of the Torah.

·

Reb Yisrael Baal Shem Tov, the founder of the Chassidic movement (1698-1760).
2 *Kesser Shem Tov,* p. 12c.
3 *Sefer HaMaamarim* of the Rebbe Rayatz, 5689; *maamar* beginning with the words "*Mah Tovu,*" dated 12-13 Tammuz.
4 *Isaiah* 21:12.

ENERGY IN THE LETTERS

In addition to the light in the letters written on printed matter (e.g., the letters in a Torah scroll), there is intrinsic light within each letter independent of it being written down on paper. These are the letters of Creation.

The *Mishnah* states:[5] "With Ten Utterances G-d created the world."

As a carpenter employs tools to build a home, so G-d utilized the twenty-two letters[6] of the *alef-beis* to form heaven and earth. They are the metaphorical wood, stone and nails, cornerposts and crossbeams of our earthly and spiritual existence.

G-d created the *alef-beis* before the creation of the world. The Maggid of Mezritch[7] explains[8] this on the basis of the first verse in the Book of *Genesis:* "בראשית ברא אלקים את השמים ואת הארץ— In the beginning G-d created the heavens and the earth." The word את, (*es*) is spelled with an *alef,* the first letter of the *alef-beis,* and a *tav,* which is the last. The fact is, את, *es,* is generally considered to be a superfluous word. There is no literal translation for it, and its function is primarily as a grammatical device. So why is "*es*" present *twice* in the very first line of the Torah? It suggests that in the beginning, it was not the heavens and the earth that were created first. It was literally the *alef-beis, alef* through *tav.* Without these letters, the very Utterances with which G-d formed the universe would have been impossible.

---

5 *Ethics of Our Fathers* 5:1.

6 Although there are thirty-two letters illustrated in the *alef-beis* chart printed below, we count only twenty-two distinct letters. Ten of the thirty-two letters are derivatives of letters and not considered wholly distinct. Five of them are the final form of the letter (i.e., final *chaf, mem, nun, pei* and *tzaddik*), another five are "hard" (gutteral) i.e.; *veis, chaf, fei, sin,* and *sav,* as compared to "soft" (mellifluous). Alternately, see beginning of *Sefer Yetzirah* and *Sefer HaSichos 5750,* p. 448.

7 A disciple and successor to Rabbi Yisrael Baal Shem Tov, the founder of the Chassidic movement and all its various Chassidic sects. Born in Russia in the early 1700's, the Maggid passed away on the 19th of Kislev, 1772.

8 *Or Torah, Remez* 3.

Furthermore, Rabbi Yisrael Baal Shem Tov explains the verse:[9] "Forever the words of G-d are hanging in the heavens." The crucial thing to realize is that G-d did not merely create the world once. His words didn't just emerge and then evaporate. Rather, G-d *continues* to create the world anew each and every moment. His words are there constantly, "hanging in the heavens." And the *alef-beis* is the foundation of this ongoing process of creation.

The Lubavitcher Rebbe, Rabbi Menachem M. Schneerson, explains[10] that the source of the twenty-two letters is even higher than that of the Ten Commandments. As it states:[11] "With you (the essence of G-d), the Jews will be blessed." בך means "with you." The *beis* (which has a *gematria* of 2) and the *kaf* (= 20) added together equals 22. Through the twenty-two letters of the *alef-beis*, the Jewish people are connected to G-d and receive all of their blessings.

ESSENCE OF THIS WORK

The essence of this work—that which makes it both unique and weaves everything together—are the teachings of my holy teacher, the Lubavitcher Rebbe, Rabbi Menachem Mendel Schneerson, whom we will address throughout this book as simply "the Rebbe." It is my sincere hope that the ideas conveyed herein have neither diluted nor misconstrued the Rebbe's true intention.

ACKNOWLEDGMENTS

Blessed are You G-d, our L-rd, King of the universe, Who has given us life, sustained us and allowed us to reach this auspicious occasion.

---

9 *Psalms* 119:89.
10 *Sefer HaSichos 5752*, vol. 2, p. 351, Vaad L'Hafotzas Sichos, NY, 1992.
11 *Genesis* 48:20.

To my wife, Shternie—you are a beacon of strength, wisdom and love. To my children Yankel, Eliyohu, Mendy, Chaya and Yehoshua Elimelech, you are my pride and joy.

Words cannot adequately express my gratitude to my parents, Reb BenZion and Bassie Raskin, for giving of themselves beyond the call of duty and for giving me everything a son could ask for; to my wife's parents, Rabbi Shmuel and Devorah Plotkin (Spiritual Leaders of Zhitomer and Berditchev), for their encouragement and inspiration; and to my grandmother, Rebbetzin Chava Hecht, for her unconditional love and directives.

To my dear late grandfather Rabbi Jacob J. Hecht, o.b.m., whose remarkable vision continues to guide me through life.

I am grateful to everyone who helped make this book a reality. To Rabbi Yonah Avtzon, the publisher of Sichos In English, and Yosef Yitzchok Turner for layout and design. To my editors, Erik Anjou, who gave not only of his pen but also of his heart toward the success of this volume, and to Rochel Chana Schilder, whose wisdom, insights and tireless efforts brought much clarity to the text. To Rabbi Michoel Seligson for citing sources and reviewing the book. A special thanks to Shoshana Brombacher Miller for her beautiful artistic renderings, and to Shlomo Khayms for a great job on the cover design.

A special thanks to the following people for their valuable insights: Henry Bar-Levov, Michael Bast, Steven Cohn, Rabbi Mutty Fogelman, Mitchel Garbow, Jason Goldfarb, Rabbi Shimon Hecht, Blanca Madani, Lawrence Obstfeld, Rabbi DovBer Pinson, Stephen Rosen (President and Founder of Congregation B'nai Avraham), Aunt Fradie Sabol, Bella Schapiro, Sara Schmerler, Karen Sebiri, Reb Simcha Weinstein, and Ed Weintrob. Finally, thanks to my second family, the entire congregation of B'nai Avraham. Your commitment and passion for Torah learning constantly inspires me to study more.

It is my hope and prayer that this book will stimulate the reader's interest to delve deeper into our holy Torah. "Great is study for it brings about action."[12] Action tops the scales of salvation and brings about the revelation of our righteous *Mashiach*.

Rabbi Aaron Leib Raskin

15 Menachem Av, 5763
The 13th *yartzeit* of my illustrious grandfather,
Rabbi Jacob J.[13] Hecht, of blessed memory

---

12 *Ethics of Our Fathers 1:17* in *Siddur Tehillat Hashem,* Kehot Publication Society, Brooklyn, NY. See also *Berachos* 17a.
13 *Toras Menachem, Menachem Tzion,* Vol. II, p. 433ff.; p. 451.

TERMINOLOGY

For the benefit of our general audience, we present you with a list of commonly used words.

Torah—The Five Books of Moses. Can also refer to the entire Written and Oral Law.

Talmud—The primary book of the Oral Law. It is the basis for *Halachah*—Jewish law and customs.

There are five[14] levels of interpretation in Jewish thought.

a) *Pshat*—basic understanding—the basis for the commentary of *Rashi* (an acronym of Rabbi Shlomo Yitzchaki [1040-1105]). *Rashi* is the foremost commentator on the Five Books of Moses.

b) *Remez*—hint—one law may provide a hint and lead to another one. Generally found in the *Talmud*.

c) *Drush*—homiletics and exegesis defining and explaining the verses of the Torah. Found in the *Midrash*.

d) *Sod*—secrets—found in numerous texts, and in particular, the *Zohar* and the writings of the *AriZal*, Rabbi Isaac Luria, a 16th-century Kabbalist. *Sod* is primarily the body of Jewish mystical thought known as *Kabbalah*.

e) *Chassidus*—essence—the fifth and highest dimension of Torah also referred to as the Teachings of *Mashiach*. *Chassidus* clarifies *Kabbalah* and imparts the underlying spiritual meaning behind the four above-mentioned levels.

PRONUNCIATION

To aid the reader in pronouncing the transliterated Hebrew words that appear in this text, we have adopted the following rules:

a, e, o, u = the short pronunciation of the vowel

aa="ah-ah" as in *yaar*, pronounced "yah-ar"

---

14 See *On the Essence of Chassidus*, page 33ff., Vaad L'Hafotzas Sichos, NY, 5747; *Sefer HaSichos 5750*, Vol. II, p. 601, fn. 64.

ai=long "i" as in *zain*, pronounced "zine"
ea="ay-ah" as in the word *meah*, pronounced "may-ah"
ei=long "a" as in *beis*, pronounced "base"
i=long "e" as in *min*, pronounced "mean"
ch=a guttural sound made by forcing air through the closure formed by the back of the tongue against the palate, as in the words Chanukah and *challah*.

Alef-Beis Chart
PRONUNCIATION AND GEMATRIA

5 **הֵ** HEI	4 **דּ** DALET	3 **גּ** GIMMEL	2 **בּ** VEIS	2 **בּ** BEIS	1 **א** ALEF
20 **כּ** KAF	10 **י** YUD	9 **ט** TES	8 **ח** CHES	7 **ז** ZAYIN	6 **ו** VAV
50 **נ** NUN	40 **ם** FINAL MEM	40 **מ** MEM	30 **ל** LAMED	20 **ך** FINAL CHAF	20 **כ** CHAF
80 **ף** FINAL FEI	80 **פּ** FEI	80 **פּ** PEI	70 **ע** AYIN	60 **ס** SAMECH	50 **ן** FINAL NUN
300 **שׂ** SIN	300 **שׁ** SHIN	200 **ר** REISH	100 **ק** KUF	90 **ץ** FINAL TZADDIK	90 **צ** TZADDIK
		400 **תּ** SAV	400 **ת** TAV		

Nekudos Chart

16 CHOLAM	20 SH'VA	30 SEGOL	20 TZEIREH	6 PATACH	16 KAMATZ
	16 MILUPIM	30 SHURUK	10 CHIRIK		

אדם

ג'

Alef

ALEF—THE DIFFERENCE BETWEEN
EXILE AND REDEMPTION

Design	A dot on top and on bottom; a line in between
Gematria	One and 26
Meaning	1. Master 2. teacher 3. wondrous

The Alter Rebbe, Rabbi Schneur Zalman of Liadi,[1] wanted to teach his son the *alef-beis*. He called one of his disciples into his study to discuss the matter. The Rebbe said, "You have a *mitzvah* and I have a *mitzvah*. Your *mitzvah* is to support your own family. My *mitzvah* is to teach my son. Let's trade *mitzvos*. You will teach my son, and I will pay you so that you can support your family." The Alter Rebbe went on to explain exactly how this instruction should proceed. "You'll begin with the letter *alef*. What is an *alef*?" The Alter Rebbe continued melodically in Yiddish: "*A pintele fun oybin, a pintele fun untin, a kav b'emtza*—[The *alef* is] a dot above, a dot below, and a diagonal line suspended in between."[2]

Design

What is an *alef*?

If it were only a random arrangement of pen strokes designed to prompt the reader to say the sound "ah,"[3] this question would be irrelevant. Every aspect of the *alef*'s construction has been Divinely designed to teach us something. Contrast this with a child learning to read English for the first time. He is never taught *why* a capital "A" looks like a teepee and a small "a" looks like a soap bubble stuck to a wall.

But Hebrew is different. The design of an *alef* is actually made up of three different letters: the letter *yud* or dot above; a

VAV → ← YUD
YUD →

yud or dot below; and a diagonal *vav*, or line suspended in between.

The *yud* above represents G-d, Who is above (or beyond) our comprehension.

---

1 1747-1812. The first Rebbe, or leader, of the Chassidic movement known alternately as *Chabad* or *Chabad* Lubavitch.

2 *HaYom Yom*, entry for 8 Adar I. Kehot Publication Society, Brooklyn, NY, 1994; See also *Likkutei Sichos*, vol. 2, p. 616, Vaad L'Hafotzas Sichos, NY.

3 The *alef* is actually an inarticulated letter whose sound is determined only by its accompanying vowel.

In comparison to His true essence, our understanding is a mere dot.

The *yud* below represents a *Yid* or *Yehudim*—Jewish people who dwell here on earth. The only way that we can grasp G-d's wisdom—to the extent that a person is capable—is by being humble. When we realize that we are but a dot or a speck compared to the All-Mighty and All-Powerful G-d, we become a vessel to receive His Divine wisdom.

The diagonal *vav* represents a Jew's faith[4]—which unites him with G-d.

There is another teaching[5] that posits that the suspended *vav* represents the Torah. Since the Torah is what unites a Jew and G-d, the *alef* represents this unity between mankind and G-d. This is the design, or form, of the *alef.*

We can see that every stroke of the *alef* (and every other letter as well) has a special purpose, and that there is much more to learning the *alef-beis* than just mastering its sounds.

Gematria

Every letter of the *alef-beis* has a numerical value, or *gematria*. The *gematria* of *alef* is one, representing the one (or oneness of) G-d, as we say in the famous prayer: "Hear, O Israel, G-d is our L-rd, *G-d is One.*"

On a more complex level, we explained that the form of the *alef* comprises three letters: two *yuds* and a *vav*. The *gematria* of the *yud* is ten—two *yuds* being twenty. A *vav* is six; the sum of all three totaling twenty-six. One of the great names of G-d is the Four Letter Name י-ה-ו-ה, the Tetragrammaton, or Ineffable Name. The *gematria* of the *Yud* (=10), the *Hei* (=5), the *Vav* (=6) and the *Hei* (=5) totals 26, the same as the *yud-vav-yud* of the

---

4 The vertical line of the *vav* represents hierarchy: the submission of a subject to his king (as explained in the chapter on the letter *hei*).

5 See chapter on the letter *vav* and Appendix 2. See also *Likkutei Sichos*, vol. 2, p. 616.

alef. Through the connection of their respective *gematrios*, the *alef* represents G-d's Ineffable Name.

Meaning

The Rebbe[6] explains that the *alef* has three different meanings. One is אלוף, *aluf*, which means a master or a chief. The second is אולפנה, *ulfana*, a school of learning[7] or teacher. The third meaning is reached by reading the letters of the word backwards—פלא, *pela* (pronounced *peleh*)—wondrous.[8]

Aluf's definition is "master." This lets the world know that there is a Creator; that G-d is the Master of the universe, and that there is an Eye that sees, and an Ear that hears. The universe did not simply emerge by itself; there is an omnipotent Force that actually forged the firmaments *ex nihilo,* from nothing to something. Thus G-d is the *Aluf,* the Master of the universe.

Ulfana means "school" or "teacher." Not only do we introduce G-d as the Creator of the universe, but also as the Teacher of all mankind. G-d's role as teacher is revealed with His introduction of Torah to the Jewish people. The Torah, with its 613 *mitzvos* or laws, teaches us what we should do, and what we shouldn't do. Through the Divine wisdom of His book, G-d establishes Himself in the world on the level of the ultimate Teacher.

Finally, we have the third meaning of *alef: peleh,* "wondrous." *Peleh* represents the esoteric or mystical level of Torah—*Kabbalah* and the teachings of Chassidic thought. Known as the "teachings of *Mashiach,*" these secrets of Torah comprise its greatest level.

---

6 *Sefer HaSichos,* 5751, vol. II, p. 523.

7 Also see *Job* 33:33—ואאלפך—"And I will 'teach' you."

8 As stated in the introduction, the letter *pei* is comprised of both a *pei* (which has the sound of "p") and a *fei* (the sound of "f"). When calculating *gematrios* or in transpositions of letters in various words, the letters are considered the same.

The Baal Shem Tov once entered *Mashiach's* heavenly chamber[9] and asked, "*Mashiach*, when are you going to come?" *Mashiach* responded, "When the wellsprings of your teachings (i.e., the teachings of *Chassidus*) spread forth throughout the entire world." Thus, only when the level of *peleh*—this level of wondrous esoteric thought—has permeated the world, will the arrival of *Mashiach* be imminent.

This can also be connected to a fundamental concept in the *Talmud*. The *Talmud* tells us[10] that G-d created the world to exist for 6,000 years.[11] The first two thousand years are called *Tohu,* or chaos. This is followed by two thousand years of Torah. And the final two thousand are the days of *Mashiach*.

What does this mean? *Rashi* explains that the first two thousand years began with the first man, Adam. This corresponds to the first meaning of the letter *alef*: *aluf*—master—for the *Midrash* states that Adam caused all the animals and beasts to bow down to G-d, thus acknowledging Him as Master and Creator of the universe. However, that era was qualified as chaos, because the Torah was not yet revealed.

The second two thousand years, *Rashi* continues, began with Abraham. Abraham introduced the Torah. As the *Talmud* states,[12] Abraham both learned and fulfilled the entire Torah long before it was physically given to the Jewish people at Mount Sinai. His embracing of G-d's word inaugurated the era of Torah—and thus the second meaning of the word *alef*—*ulfana*, or teaching.

The final two-thousand-year period is considered the days of *Mashiach*; the concept of *peleh*. This wondrous era has the po-

---

9 The introduction to *Kesser Shem Tov of the Baal Shem Tov*, Kehot Publication Society, Brooklyn, NY; *The Religious Thought of Hassidism*, Norman Lamm, Yeshiva University Press, NY, 1999, p. 550.
10 *Sanhedrin* 97a.
11 After which the world will exist in an eternal state of peace and tranquility.
12 *Yoma* 28b.

tential to usher in peace and tranquility throughout the entire world. Here, at this final level of *alef*, a teaching of the Baal Shem Tov illuminates an interesting point. The Alter Rebbe suggests that the difference between the words גולה—*golah* (exile) and גאולה—*geulah* (redemption), is the presence of the *alef*.[13] If one inserts an *alef* into the word גולה (*golah*/exile), exile is empowered and transformed into גאולה (*geulah*/redemption). Thus the final two thousand years of Creation, the era of *Mashiach*, is represented by the *alef*. Having been given the *alef*, the Jewish people are empowered to move from exile to redemption. The stages of G-d as Master of the universe and as Teacher blossom into the days of *Mashiach*, when G-d will be revealed on a wondrous level. All of this is contained in the letter *alef*.

---

13 *Likkutei Torah, Behaalos'cha*, p. 35c.

בֵּית
בִּיכֶער

נ

_____

Beis

_____

BEIS—CREATION

Design	One vertical and two horizontal lines, representing east, south, west
Gematria	Two and 412
Meaning	House

King Ptolemy II (283-246 BCE) wanted a Greek translation of the Torah (the Septuagint). He gathered 72 elders of Israel and sequestered them in 72 different houses.[1] He visited each of them and said, "Translate for me the book of Moses your teacher." Miraculously, each Sage's translation was identical even though each, independently, had made certain changes in the translation. The Jewish elders felt that if they gave Ptolemy G-d's literal words to Moses—Ptolemy might be misled or use it against the Jewish people.

Significantly, the Sages had all altered the first verse of the Torah. Instead of writing בראשית—"*Bereishis*, (In) the beginning, created G-d...," they wrote אלקים—"*Elokim* (G-d) created, (in) the beginning," thus beginning the Torah with the letter א—*alef* instead of the letter ב—*beis*.

Design

The design of the *beis*, the second letter of the *alef-beis*, comprises three lines: two horizontal and one vertical. These three lines represent the directions east, south, and west. The horizontal line on top represents the east. The vertical line is the south, and the horizontal line below is the west. The design of the *beis* is similar to the path of the sun, which rises in the east and sets in the west. The *Midrash*[2] states that the letter *beis* is similar to the construction of the world. A contemporary illustration of this is offered by geologists. When you look at the earth, you see that there are land masses to the east, west, and south. Even beneath the ice cap of the South Pole, one finds the continent of Antarctica. But beneath the frozen mass of the North Pole, there's nothing. The north is "open."

The immediate lesson we derive from the *beis* is that the world was created incomplete. The job of humankind is thus to

---

1 *Megillah* 9a.
2 *Midrash HaNe'elam* (the *Midrash* to *Song of Songs*).

complete Creation by *perfecting* it. We do this through our good deeds and by making the world a better place to inhabit.

Furthermore, north represents evil, as it states:[3] "From the north the evil will be released upon all the inhabitants of the land." G-d's declaration is in direct response to Jeremiah's vision of a bubbling pot whose opening is from the north, a vision that portends the destruction of the first Holy Temple. Babylon, the nation that destroyed the First Holy Temple, in fact, attacked from the north.

Understanding that the north represents evil is not enough: we have an obligation to fight to overcome this evil. We also need to recognize that the "open" side, this northern aspect, exists *within* the individual as well as from without. In a person, this is called the *yetzer hara*—the evil inclination, which tempts and cajoles us to sin. The only antidote is to strive to perfect oneself, which in turn contributes to the perfection of the world. This correction, or *tikkun*, of oneself—and hence the world—is embodied in the design of the letter *beis*.

Gematria

The *gematria* of *beis* is two. Two represents duality and plurality. Everything in Creation was created in pairs. Man and woman, male and female. This bifurcation informs us that we are not G-d. Only G-d can be One. But for mankind to create, to reproduce, two are required. *Beis* also represents the level of intellect, in contrast to the *alef*, which represents faith.

The commentaries on the Torah ask,[4] "Why does the Torah begin with the letter *beis* instead of an *alef*?" particularly when the *Zohar* states that the *alef* is the holiest letter (because it is first in the order of the *alef-beis*).

---

3 *Jeremiah* 1:14.
4 See *Likkutei Sichos*, vol. 15, p. 1.

The Rebbe gives the following explanation: When a person reads the beginning of the Torah, he wonders: "Why does the Torah begin with a *beis*, the second letter of the *alef-beis*? Why doesn't the Torah begin with the first letter, the *alef*?" And the answer unfolds as follows:

In *Jeremiah*[5] the question is asked: "Why was the land of Israel destroyed?" G-d answers, "Because the Jewish people have forsaken My Torah." The *Talmud*[6] counters, "What do you mean they didn't learn Torah? [The Jewish people were *constantly* studying Torah.]" The *Talmud* thus deduces that the reason the land was destroyed was that the Jews didn't make a blessing before they began to study the Torah.

What is the blessing over the Torah? "Blessed are You, G-d our L-rd, King of the universe, Who has chosen us out of all nations of the world, and given us *His* Torah [(i.e., not a man-made Torah, but dictated by G-d to Moses letter by letter; and as such, true and unchanged for all generations)], blessed are You G-d Who gives the Torah."[7]

A person must verbalize this introductory blessing every day before he begins to study Torah. Rabbi Yoel Sirkis[8] explains[9] that the purpose of Torah study is to "cleave and become one with G-d through the holiness of His word, and thereby cause the *Shechinah*, the Divine Presence of G-d, to dwell amongst us." Indeed, there are two levels to our relationship with the Torah. The first is to believe with complete faith that the Torah comes from G-d (and is therefore beyond human intellect); and the second, that it is only because of G-d's compassion and love

---

5 9:11-12.

6 *Nedarim* 81a.

7 The blessing "Who *gives* the Torah" was composed in the present tense, emphasizing that the Giving of the Torah occurs every day, and since G-d gives the Torah anew every day, it is relevant to every person in every generation.

8 Also known as the *Bach* (Poland, 1561-1640).

9 The commentary of the *Bach* on *Tur, Orach Chaim*, ch. 47.

for His people that He allows us to understand the Torah intellectually.

If one denies the divinity of Torah, one cannot properly understand its G-dly concepts. Our intellect alone is incapable of arriving at the true meaning of the Torah's contents.

Therefore, the Torah begins with a *beis*, the second letter of the *alef-beis*. This is to hint to us that when we endeavor to acquire the understanding of Torah merely with our intellect, we are lacking the primary purpose of Torah: to become one with G-d—the *Alef*.

King Ptolemy II could not have understood the message of the *beis*. He would have said that since *beis* represents intellect, then intellect must be worshiped. By beginning the Septuagint with an *Alef*—"G-d created"—the Rabbis were reflecting in effect that G-d—and not man—is the primary force in the world.[10]

In light of the above, the words of the *Jerusalem Talmud* become clear. The reason the Torah begins with a *beis* is that *beis* stands for *berachah*—blessing. If one's Torah study is preceded by the *alef*, it will be blessed with intellect and understanding.

Meaning

The meaning of *beis* is *bayis*, which is Hebrew for "home." Why did G-d create the world? The *Midrash*[11] tells us that G-d desired a home. How does one define a home? A home is the place to which you return after finishing with your worldly affairs. You remove your shoes, change to comfortable clothes, and relax. You don't have to put on a show or "sell" yourself to anyone. It's a place where the real you comes alive. G-d also wanted a place where He could be Himself and unite with His bride, the Jewish people. *That* was the objective of Creation.

10 See *Likkutei Sichos*, vol. 15, p. 3ff., for a different explanation.
11 *Tanchuma, Naso* 16.

That is the *beis* of *bayis*, the first letter of the Torah, the blueprint of Creation.

With *beis* signifying Creation, we note that the root of the word *Bereishis*—בּ-ראשׁ-ית—is *rosh*, which means head. The prefix is a *beis*. The last two letters of the word are *yud* and *tav*. Together, the *beis*, *yud* and *tav* spell *bayis*—house.[12] In the beginning, when G-d created the world, His *taavah*, תאוה (desire), was that the Head (which is G-d) should dwell in the *bayis*, His home. And how does one make a home for G-d? By living the letter *beis*. The three lines of the *beis* are often interpreted as representing the three pillars on which the world stands: Torah, prayer, and charity (including good deeds). When a person prays, studies Torah, and gives charity daily, one builds a home for G-d. The word תאוה, *taavah*, has the *gematria* of 412: *tav*=400, *alef*=1, *vav*=6, *hei*=5. If you add up the letters of the word *bayis*: *beis*=2, *yud*=10, *tav*=400, they also equal 412.[13]

The aforementioned three lines of the *beis*—the pillars of Torah, prayer, and charity (and good deeds)—also hearken back to the original three directions of its design. Since the *beis* also contains the open direction, the north, which portends evil, the very structure of the letter embodies an internal tension. Its lack of physical closure poses both an invitation and a potential danger, and they both point to the obligation of the Jewish people to complete G-d's creation, to finish His home and to perfect the world. We do this by bringing G-dliness down into the world and by acting in accordance with the *beis*, the house. We fulfill our obligations through the study of Torah, prayer, and the giving of charity. Then and only then will G-d dwell in His home, and will we truly merit a world of *berachah*, of blessing.

---

12 Rabbi Yitzchak Ginsburgh, *The Alef-Beit*, p. 39, Jason Aronson, Inc., Northvale, NJ 1992, quoting the *Hakdomas Tikkunei Zohar* 12b.

13 *Ibid.*, p. 38.

גְּיב

גֶּעלט

Gimmel

GIMMEL—CHARITY

Design	1. Rich man running 2. *vav* and *yud* 3. camel
Gematria	Three
Meaning	1. Nourish 2. weaned 3. camel 4. bridge

My mother's paternal great-grandfather, Hersh-Meilech Hecht, came to the shores of America in 1880. The story is told that one day, when Hersh-Meilech was in the *beis midrash* (study hall) of the Shiniva Rav, Rabbi Yechezkel Halberstam, the Rav placed a *pushka* (charity box) in his hand and told him: "Travel to America and become a fundraiser."[1] Sometime later, when Hersh-Meilech sent word to his wife, Ita Dreizel, to come to America, she went to the Shiniva Rav to ask his advice. The Rav's response was: "If your husband asked you to go to America, you should go." She began to cry, "How can one raise G-d-fearing children in America? It is a *treifa medina* (a non-kosher country)." The Rav then blessed her and said, "Go in peace. I guarantee you will see generations upon generations of G-d-fearing Jews, learning His Holy Torah and following in the ways of G-d."

In addition to raising money for Jews in Europe and Israel, my grandparents' home in America was always open for guests, many of whom were Rabbis and heads of schools. Before leaving, they each would receive a handsome sum for their respective *yeshivos*. Thank G-d, we still reap the fruit of the Shiniva Rav's blessing.[2]

Design

What is a *gimmel*? The letter *gimmel* represents the benefactor or the giver of charity. The design of the letter *gimmel* is explained in the *Talmud*[3] as a rich man running to give charity to a poor person.

---

1 In Yiddish, he said: *"Far kein America un ver a Gabai Tzedakah."*
2 In *Hayom Yom*, entry for 9 Tammuz, the Rebbe writes: "The greatest guaranteed assurance of Divine assistance for all Jewish parents in need of special help and deliverance for their children is through their support of those who study Torah."
3 *Shabbos* 104a.

According to *Kabbalah*,[4] the design of the *gimmel* is composed of two letters. The first is a *vav*, representing man, because he stands upright. To the man's left side is the second
letter, a *yud*, which signifies both the foot and the act of giving.
In our own lives we find that the upper body, from the waist up,
has a tendency toward selfishness, the predisposition to "take."
Our intellect often exists for itself, applying its faculties to
secure its needs. The mouth, stomach, and digestive tract are
employed in the intake of food and drink. The lower portion of
the body, however, is the part that gives to others. With our legs
we walk distances in order to help another person. Our hands
reach into our pockets to get the money to give to charity. The
yud can also represent the reproductive organ, the seedbed of
human life.

Another suggestion is that because of its long neck, the
gimmel looks like a camel.[5] According to Rabbi Samson Rafael
Hirsch,[6] the word *gimmel* is similar to the Hebrew word *gamal*,
which means "camel."[7]

Gematria

The numerical value of *gimmel* is three. The *Talmud* says that
the number three represents the Torah, which was given to the
Jewish people in the third month of the year (Sivan) to our
teacher Moses (the third of three children) on the third day of
separation between husband and wife (the prohibition of mari-
tal relations, as instructed by G-d). The Torah was issued to a
people of three groups: the *Kohanim*, the Levites and the Israelites. Finally, the Torah itself is divided into three segments: the
Five Books of Moses, the Prophets and the Scriptures.[8]

---

4 *The Alef-Beit, op. cit.,* p. 54.
5 Rabbi Michael L. Munk, *The Wisdom in the Hebrew Alphabet*, p. 71, Mesorah Press, Brooklyn,
   NY, 1983.
6 Major figure and great leader of German Jewry (1808-1888).
7 In his commentary on *Genesis* 21:8.
8 *Shabbos* 88a.

R. Yehudah Loew (the *Maharal* of Prague)[9] explains that the power of the number three is its ability to combine two contrasting forces—to bring about integration.[10] What does this mean? Let's say a person is born into the world of Torah. He grows up in a cloistered society. He goes to *yeshivah* all his life and all he knows is G-d. Finally, this person gets married and goes out into the mundane world and begins to earn a living. He says, "Hey, there's a materialistic world out here! There are things besides G-dliness, besides spirituality. Maybe there are in fact *two* realities. The first reality is G-d. Then there's a second reality, the world. And these realities contradict each other...." Therefore, Torah is given in the third month because "three" has the power to merge G-dliness with the mundane world. For example, our Sages state: "If there is no bread, there is no Torah."[11] G-d *expects* us to make a living in order to support our loved ones and give charity. And by conducting our worldly affairs according to Torah—with honesty and integrity— we are actually finding G-d in the physical world.

There is a story told of Aristotle's student, Alexander the Great, who one day entered his master's home unannounced. To his astonishment, Alexander found Aristotle engaged in immoral behavior. Later, when they were alone, Alexander asked, "Is *this* the way of the great Aristotle—the philosopher, the teacher, the mentor? Is *this* proper ethical behavior?!" Aristotle responded, "When I teach you philosophy and the wonders of the world, I'm Aristotle. But here, in private, I'm not Aristotle."

This story stands in stark contrast to the character of Rabbi Akiva[12] and the Torah he embodied. Rabbi Akiva would often be summoned by the Roman official Tinus Rufis for a spirited de-

---

9 1526-1609.

10 *Tiferes Yisroel*, ch. 18, written by the *Maharal*. See also *Likkutei Sichos*, vol. 2, p. 301ff.

11 *Ethics of Our Fathers* 3:17.

12 One of our history's greatest Sages. He died as a martyr (135 C.E.) at the hands of the Romans nearly 65 years after the destruction of the Second Temple.

bate.[13] In the end, Rabbi Akiva always outsmarted him. One day
Rafina, the wife of Tinus Rufis, decided to avenge her husband's
honor. Knowing that the G-d of the Hebrews forbade immorality, she won Tinus Rufis' permission to seduce Rabbi Akiva and
thus cause him to sin. The next time Rabbi Akiva was summoned to the palace, Rafina hid behind one of the trees in the
garden. As Rabbi Akiva approached, she walked out in front of
him, dressed provocatively. Now, Rafina was a very beautiful
woman, and she was sure that Rabbi Akiva would surrender to
her charms. But the Sage proceeded to do the following: first he
spat, then he laughed, then he cried. Rafina was completely
stunned. She asked him to explain his actions. Rabbi Akiva
answered, "Two I'll tell you, and the third I won't. I spat because
of your 'despicable actions.'[14] I cried because I know that one
day your beautiful form will lie in the dust and decompose. As
to why I laughed, perhaps one day you will understand."

What is the connection between the stories of Aristotle and
Rabbi Akiva? Aristotle separated body and spirit, but Rabbi
Akiva considered them inseparable. For Aristotle, that which
was "spiritual" (i.e., the intellect and the sciences) was holy.
That which was corporeal, of the body, was profane. The two
realms were not connected and occupied two different spheres
of intention. Rabbi Akiva, however, lived by the *gimmel*, the
merger of G-d and the world. Rabbi Akiva saw G-d in *everything*, and recognized that G-d resides even in the physical.
Therefore, Rabbi Akiva had the ability to control and overcome
the temptation of Rafina. Rafina later converted to Judaism and
married Rabbi Akiva. This prophetic foresight was the reason
for his laughter.

---

13 *Nedarim* 50b; see commentaries there.
14 Rabbi Akiva was alluding to the literal translation of the *mishnah* in *Ethics of Our Fathers* 3:1
    which refers to a person's origin being "from a putrid drop."

Meaning

Gimmel has several meanings.[15] One is to nourish until ripe. After Korach rebelled against Moses and Aaron,[16] G-d told Moses, "Take a staff from Aaron and from all the other tribes of Israel. Then place the staves in the Holy of Holies [and see which one actually sprouts fruit]." The next morning, Moses brought out the staves from the Holy of Holies, and all of Israel saw that the staff of Aaron produced (*vayigmal*) completely ripened almonds. Thus the word *vayigmal*–ויגמל–is comprised of the letters גימל–*gimmel*.

Another meaning of *gimmel* is "to be weaned": "The child [Isaac] grew and was weaned (*vayigamal*)."[17] At first glance, the concepts of being weaned and nourished until ripe seem contradictory. When you're nourishing, you are giving. When you're weaning, you are ceasing to give. In essence, however, they are consistent, because if you nourish until ripe, you no longer have to give.

As mentioned, the *gimmel* is also called *gamal*, or camel. The camel itself embodies the process of weaning and nourishing, as it is able to sustain itself on journeys of vast distances after being sufficiently watered. We also note that *gimmel* is similar to the word *gomel*, to be kind or benevolent. The camel is able to help the sojourner survive the harsh desert sun by carrying him to his destination. The word *gimmel* in Aramaic is *gamla*, or bridge. One can say that the bridge is the humpback of the camel itself, which provides the means and structure to bring people where they need to go.

Now, how is it that the *gimmel* actually signifies the wealthy man running after the pauper? The answer can be found perhaps in the difference between the terms "charity" and "*tzeda-*

---

15 *The Wisdom in the Hebrew Alphabet, ibid.*
16 *Numbers* 17:17-24.
17 *Genesis* 21:8.

kah." Charity means that you are a benefactor. You are a prominent and wealthy man and you take pity on and grant mercy to this poor, homeless person by giving him charity.

Tzedakah, in contrast, has a fundamentally different meaning. The definition of *tzedakah* is righteousness or justice—simply put, to do the right thing.[18] In the case of *tzedakah*, your money doesn't really belong to you; G-d loaned it to you[19] so that when a poor person comes along, you can give him his money. You even have an obligation to run after him and "return" the money; it never belonged to you in the first place. Furthermore, one gives *tzedakah* because G-d rewards measure for measure. In order for one to receive G-d's blessing, one needs to do for others.

The act of *tzedakah* goes one step further still. You're obligated to create a bridge between the poor person and yourself. You shouldn't remain two separate, segregated entities. There has to be a merger. The greatest level of charity is not to give a person a few dollars, a one-time gift, and then say, "Goodbye, I'll never see you again." The greatest level of charity is to set a person on his feet, nourish him until he's ripe, and then wean him so that he never has to ask for money again. This is done by putting him into business, or by giving him a job.

This is the concept of *gimmel*; the blending of disparate elements into a harmonious whole. Just as the *gimmel* signifies the connection between the poor and the wealthy person, so does it represent the merger, the bridge, between the material world and the reality of G-d.

---

18 *Likkutei Sichos,* vol. 2, p. 410.

19 Why couldn't G-d just give the money to the poor man Himself? Because G-d desires a world in which people are kind to others, in which people reach out to those less fortunate than they. G-d will then be obligated to mirror His children's actions and thus give abundantly to them (*Shmos Rabbah* 31:5). See also *Likkutei Sichos,* vol. 3, p. 909.

ד

דלות   דלת

Dalet

DALET—PASSOVER

Design	1. Leg extends to *gimmel*
	2. door post and lintel 3. *yud* and *reish*
Gematria	Four
Meaning	1. Poor 2. door 3. lift up

A young girl is born into an observant Jewish home. A staunch believer, she wakes up one morning and suddenly decides she wants to experience other religions. So she explores various cults and faiths, and begins to learn about their ideas. Her father, of course, is puzzled. There is a rabbi nearby, an emissary (*shaliach*) of the Rebbe. So the father asks him for advice. The *shaliach* answers: we'll write to the Rebbe—since the Rebbe is known for his prophetic vision and his love for every Jew—and see what he tells us. The pair composes a letter to the Rebbe and the Rebbe replies, "Check your *mezuzahs.*" The father and the *shaliach* proceed to take off the many *mezuzahs* in the house. The father is a very wealthy man. He's the *gimmel*, the giver. They bring the *mezuzahs* to a scribe to be checked. But there's nothing wrong with them. Each one is perfect. Time goes on and the girl is becoming more and more steeped in foreign faiths. Again the father and the *shaliach* write to the Rebbe: "What should we do?" The Rebbe answers a second time, "Check your *mezuzahs.*" So the men remove the *mezuzahs* a second time and check them from top to bottom, but again they're perfect. But if the Rebbe says, "Check the *mezuzahs*," what are they to do?

One day the *shaliach* is strolling with the father across his beautiful property, some seven acres in size. At the end of a field the rabbi notices a small hut. He asks, "Does this belong to you?" The father replies that it does. "Does it have a *mezuzah*?" "Well, we put one there many years ago." So the two men check the *mezuzah* on the door of the hut and, in the first verse of the *Shema*, where it is meant to read אחד, *echad* (one), part of the *dalet* has been rubbed away and it reads אחר, *acher* (other). They immediately replace the *mezuzah*, and the following morning the daughter wakes up crying. "Daddy, I'm sorry. I don't know what happened to me. I don't

know what got into me. But I want to return. I want to come
home to Judaism."

Design

The *dalet* is the fourth letter of the *alef-beis*. The *Talmud*[1] tells
us that the *dalet* represents the poor person. Thus the phrase
gomel dalim: the benefactor who gives to the beneficiary.

The *Talmud*[2] also tells us that when we observe the shape of
the *dalet*, its single leg stretches toward the right—in the
direction of the *gimmel*. This teaches the poor person that he
has to make himself available to receive the charity of the
benefactor. Similarly,[3] the small extension on the right-hand
side of the *dalet's* horizontal bar looks like an ear, for the
pauper must always be listening for the presence of the wealthy
man. However the left side of this bar doesn't confront the
gimmel, the giver, but faces left, toward the letter *hei*, which
represents G-d. This instructs us that we must give charity
discretely and not embarrass the poor person. The pauper must
put his faith in G-d, Who is the ultimate Giver of the universe.

The *Mishnah*[4] tells us that in the Holy Temple, there was a
room called "the Silent Chamber." One would enter this room
alone and close the door directly behind him. In the room was a
big box. One had a choice: either to put money into the box or
to take some out. Of course, the rich man would put money in.
And after him, also alone, would come the poor man, who took
money out. It was all done discreetly. The rich man couldn't see
to whom he was giving charity. The poor person didn't know
from whom he was taking it.

---

1 *Shabbos* 104a.
2 *Ibid.*
3 *The Wisdom in the Hebrew Alphabet, op. cit.,* p. 80.
4 *Shekalim* 5:6.

A second approach to the form or design of the *dalet* is that the *dalet* represents a doorpost and a lintel.[5] The vertical line is the doorpost; the horizontal line is the lintel. What is the connection between the door and the poor man? Customarily, a poor man must knock on doors.

There's also a third interpretation provided by the teachings of *Chassidus*.[6] This view points out that the *dalet* is composed of a *reish* and a *yud*. What's the difference between the *dalet*, ד and the *reish*, ר? A *yud*. If one affixes a *yud* to the upper right-hand corner of the *reish*, the *reish* becomes a *dalet*. The *yud*, a very small letter, represents humility. That humility is what separates the *reish* from the *dalet*. The *mezuzah* on our doorposts contains the famous paragraph of the prayer known as the *Shema*. In the *Shema* we say, "Hear O Israel, G-d is our L-rd, G-d is One." The word *echad*, one, as in "G-d is One," is spelled with the letters *alef, ches, dalet*, אחד. What happens if the *yud* is removed from the *dalet* and it becomes a *reish*? The word is no longer *echad*, but *acher*, אחר—other. If such a mistake were made, this would now translate into, "Hear O Israel, G-d is our L-rd, G-d is other (i.e., other gods)." So critical is the aspect of *yud*, humility, in the belief in G-d's oneness that its omission might cause one to reject G-d, G-d forbid, and believe in the existence of other omnipotent powers in the universe. The *Midrash*[7] tells us that if one switches the *reish* for the *dalet*, he's destroying all the worlds.

Gematria

The *gematria* of *dalet* is four. Four represents the Matriarchs: Sarah, Rebecca, Rachel, and Leah. It also represents the four created worlds as explained in *Kabbalah*: *Atzilus, Beriah,*

---

5 *The Wisdom in the Hebrew Alphabet, op. cit.,* p. 78, which cites the *Maharal.*
6 *Basi LeGani 5710,* ch. 6, Kehot 1990. p. 28ff. (English edition).
7 *Vayikra Rabbah* 19:2.

Yetzirah and *Asiyah*. In addition, *dalet* signifies the four basic elements of Creation: fire (energy), air (gas), water (liquid) and earth (solid). Four also represents the holiday of Passover: the four cups of wine, the four children, the four questions.

What is the reason we drink four cups of wine on Passover?

There are four expressions of redemption in the Torah. When G-d took the Jewish people out of Egypt, He said: "I will take you out"; "I will save you"; "I will redeem you"; and finally "I will take you to Me as a nation."[8] The first three expressions involve the intervention of G-d Himself in taking the Jewish people out of Egypt. The Jews themselves remained passive. But the fourth—to become G-d's nation—required both personal and communal action on the part of the Jewish people.

What does it mean to become G-d's nation and how do we prepare ourselves? By purifying ourselves. The *Zohar*[9] tells us that at the time of the Exodus, the Jewish people were at the forty-ninth level of impurity. Had they remained in Egypt one more moment they would have fallen to the fiftieth and lowest level and been lost forever. It wasn't because of their merits, their goodness or their kindness that they deserved to be redeemed. Rather it was due to G-d's benevolence: "I will take you out," "I will save you," "I will redeem you." But how did G-d *ultimately* redeem the Jewish people? By making them His nation and by giving them His Torah. This fourth term of redemption did not occur until *Matan Torah*, when G-d gave the Torah to the Jewish people. *Matan Torah* took place forty-nine days after the Jews left Egypt. For forty-nine days, we prepared ourselves to be fit to be His people. In the first three steps of redemption, we were passive and undeserving. The fourth level we had to earn.

8 *Exodus* 6:6-8.
9 *Zohar Chadash*, beginning of *Yisro*. Also *Tzror HaMor, Bo* 12:40.

The difference between the first three and the fourth expressions is signified by the difference between matzah and wine.[10] Matzah is a food that has no taste. According to *halachah*, matzah for the Passover Seder is made simply by mixing flour and water together—called "poor man's bread." When the Jewish people were taken out of Egypt, we were in a state of spiritual poverty, undeserving of the redemption. We were like matzah, tasteless. But over the next forty-nine days, we worked on ourselves. We began to comprehend and internalize what Judaism and Torah are all about. We lifted ourselves up from the forty-nine levels of impurity to the forty-nine levels of understanding. We acknowledged G-d. Once we began to understand what Judaism embodied, once we understood what it meant to become G-d's people, we became joyous. It is for this reason that we drink wine, for it says,[11] "There is no song without wine." We drink wine so that we can fully acknowledge our redemption from Egypt and sing G-d's praises with great joy.

Matzah represents the first three expressions—G-d's intervention on behalf of the Jewish people when they were "flat," passive. The four cups of wine represent the fourth expression— becoming a nation, the active role and commitment of the Jews.

There's another way to differentiate between the three matzahs and the four cups of wine. Three represents potential; four represents the development of that potential.

In the liberation of the Jews from Egypt, G-d represents three: investing His potential in the Jewish people with the three expressions of redemption. Four represents the Jewish people, who complete the process.

---

10 *Likkutei Sichos*, vol. 26, p. 44ff. See also *Gevuros Hashem* of the *Maharal*, ch. 60.
11 *Berachos* 35a.

Potential (three) can also be represented by the father, the investor of potential, with the developer (four) represented by the mother.

We can now understand why there were three fathers and four mothers. The father (the investor of the potential) provides the seed, and the mother (the developer) takes and refines it. The father is the biological benefactor and the mother the biological beneficiary. The father is therefore represented by three. The three Patriarchs are the *gimmel*, the giver, the third letter of the *alef-beis*. The mother, the receiver and beneficiary, is represented by the *dalet*, the four Matriarchs. Once the potential is realized (i.e., the child is born), one can rejoice. The symbol of rejoicing is wine, represented by four and corresponding to the four mothers.

So the mother not only receives the seed, she develops it. In practical terms, one must first acknowledge the kernel of an idea in order to expound on it. At the Pesach Seder we acknowledge the fact that G-d took us out of Egypt. We thank G-d by drinking four cups of wine, asking four questions, and speaking about the four children. With four, we appreciate all that has happened to bring us to this day—including our own participation in bringing it to a new level. But to represent G-d's participation alone in taking us out of Egypt, we eat only three matzahs. For at the moment when G-d took us out, the future of the Jewish people lay only in potential. We were in a state of matzah; inactive vessels in a state of spiritual poverty. Through our efforts, we brought three to four—potential to actuality.

Meaning

The meaning of *dalet* is *delet*, a "door." It also means *dal*, a poor person. Finally the word *dalet* represents *dilisoni*, which means "to lift me up." How do these three definitions work together?

The convergence occurs when *every* individual realizes that he or she is poor. This poverty doesn't necessarily denote a state of financial want. Rather it means that everything a person "owns" in fact belongs to G-d. G-d has been kind enough to give us life. G-d has been kind enough to give us sustenance. Without G-d, we have nothing. The acknowledgment of this is the door into G-d's chamber. And once we enter that chamber G-d will lift us up—*dilisoni*—to bless us with life, health, sustenance and success. In Psalm 30 of the *Book of Psalms,* King David tells us, "I praise G-d because He lifts me up (*dilisoni*)." If we turn this phrase around, we could say *dilisoni*—"Because G-d lifts me up, I praise Him." In this expression, G-d lifts me up by giving me the skills to be productive. This enables me to praise Him from a higher level.

Hei

HEI—THE DEED

Design	1. The width and height of *dalet*, plus *yud*, equals spirituality 2. thought, speech, action 3. *hei* vs. *ches*
Gematria	Five
Meaning	1. Here is 2. to be disturbed 3. behold

In the late 1920's my paternal grandfather and namesake, R. Aharon Leib, went to the sixth Lubavitcher Rebbe, Rabbi Yosef Yitzchak Schneersohn, for a *berachah*, a blessing.

The blessing he requested was that his children grow up to be G-d-fearing and righteous.

The Rebbe responded: "A *berachah* is similar to rain. One must first prepare the soil by plowing and sowing. After that, G-d helps; there begins to rain 'a rain of blessing,' and then the crops grow."

Design

The fifth letter of the *alef-beis* is the *hei*.

The *Maharal*[1] tells us that the design of the *hei* is comprised of a *dalet* and a *yud*. The *dalet* is composed of one horizontal line (signifying width) and another that is vertical (signifying height), which together represent the physical world, the world of materialism. The *yud* (the detached left leg) represents G-d, and thus spirituality. The *Maharal* teaches us that just as the *dalet* and the *yud* come together to form the *hei*, so, too, one has an obligation to imbue and sanctify the physical world with spirituality and G-dliness.

In Chassidic thought,[2] the *hei* represents thought, speech and action. Just as the form of the *hei* is composed of three lines, so do thought, speech and action comprise the three garments of the soul, the three garments through which we express ourselves.

The top horizontal line (thought), by its very design, represents the concept of equality. To truly experience every person as equal, one must restructure one's thought process. Perhaps it appears on the surface that some people are better and some are worse than others. But our responsibility is to focus instead on

---

1 *The Wisdom in the Hebrew Alphabet, op. cit.*, p. 86.
2 *Basi LeGani 5710*, ch. 8 (English edition).

the soul, the G-dly spark within each person.[3] Since our souls
emanate from the same Source, we are all equal in our essence.
When we delve beneath the personality and externality of a
person and go straight to his or her core, we experience that we
are all one.

The *hei's* right vertical line represents hierarchy, which is
speech. A king rules with his words.[4] He is empowered to sit in
his palace and utter a decree, which then becomes law. People
do not have to see him. He does not have to shake their hands.
All he needs to do is speak; that is his power. The vertical line
of the *hei* descends from a higher state, the ruler, to a lower
state, his subjects.

Finally, the shorter, detached leg on the left side of the *hei*
represents action. Why is this limb detached? It is very easy for
us to think and speak about what is right, but it is quite another
thing to bring a good intention to fruition. Therefore, the gap
serves as a reminder of the effort that is required to unify all
three garments. Without the line of action, we're left with the
two lines of the *dalet:* poverty.

The *Talmud*[5] informs us that the *hei* also represents
teshuvah—repentance. To appreciate how the form of the letter
hei embodies the concept of *teshuvah*, compare the *hei*, ה, to the
ches, ח,[6] the eighth letter of the *alef-beis*. Both forms look very
much alike. Each is made up of three lines. The one conspicuous
difference is the small aperture atop the *hei's* left limb. What
does this have to do with *teshuvah*? G-d declares to Cain after
he kills his brother Abel, "Sin (*chatas*) lies at your door."[7] The
opening (or door) on the bottom of both the *hei* and the *ches*
represents sin. With the *ches*, there can be no escape from the

3 *Tanya*, ch. 32.
4 *Ecclesiastes* 8:4.
5 *Shabbos* 104a.
6 *Likkutei Sichos*, vol. 1, p. 129ff.
7 *Genesis* 4:7.

"door of sin" without transgression (i.e., without exiting through the bottom of the *ches*). But the *hei* has another opening, another possible course of action. The little opening at the top of the *hei* allows for the possibility of *teshuvah*, or return.[5]

The difference between the *ches* and the *hei* can also be illustrated by comparing *chametz* (leaven) and matzah. Compare the spellings of the two words: *Chametz* is spelled חמצ,[8] *ches, mem, tzaddik.* Matzah is spelled מצה, *mem, tzaddik, hei.* The difference between *chametz* and matzah is the letter *ches* versus the *hei. Chametz*, leaven, represents being puffed up, the ego.[9] Matzah is flat, representing subservience, selflessness, and humility. If a person is humble, he will come to repent, to do *teshuvah.* But if a person is an egotist, he will never return to G-d. What is his attitude? "What do I need G-d for? I'm doing great on my own. Look how successful I am." Or if he wants to get away with bad behavior he might say, "What do you want from me? I'm only human. If G-d wanted me to be perfect, He would have made me that way. G-d gave me a *yetzer hara*, an evil inclination. He *set it up* so that I should sin. So why should I do *teshuvah*?" The egotist has no reason to repent. He is stuck in his ways and cannot admit his faults. The egotist is bloated with the *ches* of *chametz*, of leaven. The *hei* on the other hand is like matzah: flat and altruistic. Its very design contains an opening, a gap for an individual to pass through if he is humble. The *hei* is a human being's adoption of humility, the gateway to repentance.

In a broader sense, we need to understand that *teshuvah* does not only involve regret for commission of a sin, it means returning to one's essential self. As such, *teshuvah* is relevant for every individual, even the rare individual who has never sinned.

---

8 The word is actually spelled with the final form of the *tzaddik*: חמץ; the above spelling is used to facilitate the comparison with the word "matzah."

9 See *Osios deRabbi Akiva* on the letter *ches*. According to Rabbi Akiva, the letter *ches* itself represents ego.

The *Zohar*[10] tells us that when *Mashiach* comes, he will cause even the righteous to repent. Every person will realize that no matter what his level, he can always be better. He can constantly come closer and closer to G-d. One can accomplish this by perfecting his thought, speech and action. As man perfects himself, "G-d helps; there begins to rain 'a rain of blessing,' and the crops begin to grow."

Gematria

The numerical value of *hei* is five. Not only does the *hei* represent the garments of thought, speech and action, but these garments comprise a total of five elements:[11] two levels of thought, imaginative and meditative; two levels of speech, the words of the heart and the words of the lips; and one level of action. Why does action only have one level? Because when it comes to action, you either do something or you don't. Therefore, in the design of the *hei*, the line representing action (the separate vertical segment of the *hei*) is half a line.

Five also signifies the five levels of the soul: *nefesh*, *ruach*, *neshamah*, *chayah* and *yechidah*.[12] The fifth tier, *yechidah*, means union. People commonly refer to this level of the soul as the *pintele Yid*, the G-dly spark that every Jew possesses. The *pintele Yid* is the spark that can never become contaminated or extinguished, the spark that unites every Jew with G-d.

The *pintele Yid* is also the propelling force behind *mesirus nefesh*, self-sacrifice. This concept of self-sacrifice makes it possible for a Jew to give his life to G-d even though he has never practiced or felt consciously connected to Jewish law or custom. A Jew who has violated the Shabbos or eaten non-kosher food, who has never had a *mezuzah* on his door or given

---

10 III, 153b.

11 *The Alef-Beit, op. cit.,* p. 84.

12 *Bereishis Rabbah* 14:9, also see *On the Essence of Chassidus,* p. 23, fn. 37 and additional references there.

a penny to charity, is also the Jew who, when faced with the ultimatum "your G-d or your life," is willing to give up his life for G-d. This revelation is astonishing. How is it possible that this non-observant Jew is suddenly willing to give up his life for G-d? *Mesirus nefesh* makes sense for someone like Abraham or Rabbi Akiva, who learned Torah all their lives. But what of the person who has never opened a Jewish book and doesn't know that you read Hebrew from right to left? The answer is the *pintele Yid.* This fundamental connection to G-d is intrinsic to his being and can never be severed.

When it comes to a *mitzvah* such as keeping kosher, the non-observant Jew says to himself, "If I don't eat kosher, what's the big deal? G-d is *spiritual.* Why should He really care what I eat as long as I'm a good person? If I eat pork, surely that won't sever my relationship with G-d." Or perhaps he says, "So what if I don't go to *shul* on Shabbos and mow my lawn instead! The rabbi's sermon is boring anyway. Of course this isn't severing my relationship with G-d. G-d will forgive me. He'll understand." *But,* when it comes to giving up his religion, this same Jew recognizes that there's no room for ambivalence. "Obviously G-d would *not* forgive me for abandoning my faith. I'd be clearly stating that I don't love or believe in Him. If that's the case, I'm willing to give up my life rather than give up my G-d." This is the essential core of *teshuvah.* The reason we have an awakening to return is because of the *yechidah* level of the soul. This spark of the soul ignites the rest of our being, fueling its return to G-d.

The number five also represents redemption. In the Pesach Seder there is a fifth cup of wine called the cup of Elijah the Prophet. Elijah, the harbinger of the Redemption, will tell us to do *teshuvah,* for *Mashiach* is about to come. This promise is also represented by the expression in the Torah:[13] " I will bring

13 *Exodus* 6:8.

you into the land [of Israel]." The *Rambam*[14] tells us that when all of the Jewish people do *teshuvah*, we will be immediately redeemed.[15]

Meaning

The word *hei* has three meanings: The first is "here is," as in the verse, "Here is seed for you"[16] (*hei lachem zera*).[17] The next is "to be disturbed," as it states in Daniel[18] "And I Daniel was disturbed....(*nih'yeisi*)" And the third is "behold"[19] as in "Behold, this is our G-d...," (*hinei Elokeinu...*) which refers to beholding a revelation. These three definitions converge. When we're born and come into this world, G-d gives us seeds (i.e., the potential to be productive and make good of our lives). Many times, however, we become disturbed and confused and lose sight of our objectives. Eventually, though, every Jew will come to do *teshuvah* and acknowledge his Creator. He will then behold the revelation of G-d.

By elevating one's thought and speech and translating them into action, one reveals the *yechidah*, the fifth level and spark of *Mashiach* within his soul,[20] and this will bring us to the ultimate Redemption.

---

14 Rabbi Moses ben Maimon, also known as Maimonides (1135-1204).

15 *Mishneh Torah, Laws of Teshuvah* 7.5.

16 *Genesis* 47:23.

17 Based on the above verse, Rabbi Avraham Eliyahu Plotkin, o.b.m. (1888-1948, paternal grandfather of the author's wife), explains the following: "Why is it that Sarai, (שרי) the wife of Abraham, could not beget a child until her name was changed to Sarah (שרה) (ending with the letter *hei*)? The reason is that *hei* is needed for seed, i.e., children." Similarly we find that the names of the other Matriarchs concluded with a *hei* as well: Rivkah, (רבקה) Leah, (לאה), Zilpah, (זלפה), and Bilhahh, (בלהה). Rachel's maidservant had an extra *hei* which [she lent to] Rachel. Therefore, Rachel also conceived and begot children.

18 8:27.

19 *Isaiah* 25:9.

20 *Maor Einayim*, end of *parshas Pinchas*. Also see *Sefer HaSichos 5751*, vol. 2, p. 590 and additional references there.

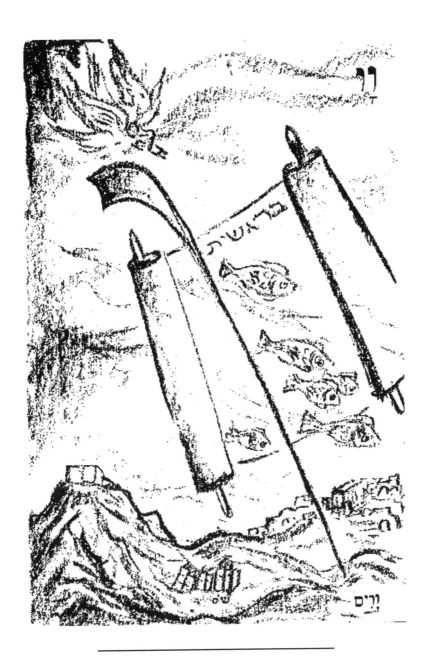

Vav

VAV—CONNECTION

Design	Hook and chute
Gematria	Six
Meaning	1. Hook, 2. the word "and," 3. in front of a word, transforms past into future or future to past

The part of the river used as a *mikveh* for ritual immersion was situated high atop a steep hill on the outskirts of Premishlan. When the road leading up to it was slippery, people had to take the long way around the hill, for to walk straight uphill was dangerous. Reb Meir, the Rebbe of Premishlan, always took the direct route up, irrespective of the state of the road, and was never known to stumble or slip. One snowy day, when the icy mountain paths were especially hazardous, Reb Meir walked uphill to the river as usual. Two guests were staying in the area, sons of the rich, who had come somewhat under the influence of the *Haskalah* or "Enlightenment" movement. These young men did not believe in supernatural achievements, and when they saw Reb Meir striding uphill with sure steps as usual, they convinced themselves and each other that the road up there was no doubt easily scaled, and not in the least dangerous. In order to prove their theory, they waited until Reb Meir had begun immersing in the river, and then set out confidently up the icy hillside road. After only a few steps on the treacherous trail, they slipped and tumbled down the path, requiring medical attention for their injuries. When one of the young men was fully healed, he mustered the courage to approach the *tzaddik* with a question: "Why was it that no one could negotiate the slippery road, while the Rebbe walked with sure steps, never stumbling?"

Reb Meir replied: "If a man is connected on high, he doesn't fall down below. Meir is tied up on high, and that is why he can take even a slippery hill in his stride."[1]

Design
The sixth letter of the *alef-beis* is the *vav*.

1 From *A Treasury of Chassidic Tales*, Rabbi Shlomo Yosef Zevin, Mesorah Publications, Ltd., NY, 1980; 1992.

The design of the letter *vav* is a hook.[2] The form of the *vav* can also represent a chute which connects a higher level to a lower level.

Gematria

The numerical equivalent of the *vav* is six. Six represents connection, exemplified by the angels in Ezekiel's vision, whose six wings enabled them to soar to unite and connect with G-d. Six also represents the six books of the *Mishnah*. Through learning Torah, one connects with G-d.

Six also represents completion, because something that is surrounded on all six sides—north, south, east, west, above and below—is complete. Similarly we find that when the Jewish people left the land of Egypt, G-d surrounded them with six Clouds of Glory.[3] The cloud above them protected them from the sun. The cloud below shielded them from the hot desert sand. The four clouds around them—back and front, left and right—served as a protective shield. Arrows and other weapons directed against them were turned to straw. In addition,[4] the Clouds of Glory also acted as "tailor" and "dry cleaner." Every night the Jewish people would remove their clothes before going to sleep. The next morning those clothes were perfectly cleaned and pressed. If a person happened to gain a few pounds, his vestments "grew" with him. The Jews wore the same clothes every day for their entire sojourn in the desert. The clothes adapted to each person's body and never grew old or worn.

The number six also signifies the six hundred thousand Jewish men aged 20-60 who left the land of Egypt. It additionally

---

2 *The Wisdom in the Hebrew Alphabet, op. cit.,* p. 84.

3 See *Rashi* on *Numbers* 10:34 where he explains that a seventh Cloud went before them, leveling the mountains and killing the snakes and scorpions in their path. See also *Likkutei Sichos,* vol. 18, p. 253ff.

4 *Rashi* on *Deuteronomy* 8:4.

represents the Torah because the word ישראל, *Yisrael*, is an acronym meaning "יש ששים רבוא אותיות לתורה—There are six hundred thousand letters of the Torah," and if *one* letter of the Torah is missing or broken or cracked, G-d forbid, the entire Torah scroll is declared not kosher—unfit to be read. Similarly, if one Jew strays from the path, or is missing or defiled, the entire Jewish nation is likewise lacking or defiled. We are rendered incomplete.

We find another instance of "six" when the Jewish people were in Egypt and oppressed with backbreaking work. Pharaoh devised many plots against the Jewish people to keep them from multiplying. Yet the Jews continued to propagate at an unbelievable rate. Indeed, the Torah tells us that the Jewish women bore six children at one time.[5]

The world was created in six days—the Six Days of Creation. The first word in the Torah is *Bereishis* ("In the beginning") which itself is composed of six letters, בראשית. Furthermore the Torah clearly states: "G-d created six days."[6] There are also six *alefs* in the first verse of the Torah. The first *vav* in the Torah is found at the beginning of the sixth word (*v'es*). So Creation is connected to the number six.

Each of these six days was created with a different emotional attribute.[7] Additionally, the progression of these six days is consistent with the *Talmud's* assertion (discussed in the chapter on *alef*) that G-d created the world (as we know it) to exist for 6,000 years. If we look into each day of Creation, we can observe each of the six millennia and its corresponding attribute.

The First Day of Creation was *Chessed*—the attribute of kindness. This was the day G-d said, "Let there be light." This light

---

5 *Rashi* on *Exodus* 1:7.
6 *Exodus* 20:11.
7 Based on *Maamarei Admur HaZakein, Parshios of the Torah and the Festivals*, p. 419; also see *Ramban* on *Genesis* 2:3, and *Likkutei Sichos*, vol. 2, pp. 466-468.

was an infinite light, a light that a person could potentially have used to see from one end of the world to the other. Eventually, however, G-d reclaimed this light, for He recognized its potential to also be used for evil. One could well ask, "How could there be light on the First Day when the sun and moon weren't formed until the Fourth Day of Creation?" The light referred to here is G-d's conception of light as the source of ultimate power, vision, potential and goodness.[8] Additionally, in the first thousand years (corresponding to the First Day), the people had enormous lifespans (Adam, for example, lived 930 years). The concept of *Chessed* thus represents G-d's kindness in both creating the infinite light and endowing man's vitality.

The Second Day of Creation was imbued with *Gevurah,* contraction and judgment. This was the day on which G-d separated the pervasive waters into the higher and lower realms. Historically, the Second Millennium saw harsh judgment leveled against the inhabitants of the world. This period was replete with difficulties, beginning with the Flood, which G-d summoned to destroy the entire world (outside of Noah and the inhabitants of the ark). This period also included the devastating episode of the Tower of Babel. An entire generation rebelled against G-d, building a tower to ascend to G-d's throne to destroy Him. G-d consequently "confounded their language,"[9] giving the people a cacophony of seventy languages to prevent them from conversing with one another. The resulting muddle, called *bavel* or "Babel," means confused or obscured.

The Third Day of Creation was a day of *Tiferes*—beauty and mercy.[10] On this day, the flowers and grasses were created, together with all the colors of the universe. The Third Millen-

---

8 This light was stored away and later given to the *tzaddikim* (the righteous people) of each generation as Divine spirit to perceive the future and the past, and to reconcile various problems and difficulties.

9 *Genesis* 11:7-9.

10 Regarding this day of Creation, the Torah states the words *ki tov* ("it was good") twice.

nium saw G-d's merciful hand in the redemption of the Jewish people from Egypt and the Giving of the Torah. The Torah is called *Tiferes*, or beauty. Beauty is not monochromatic or monotonal; it is created by blending and harmonizing various colors or sounds. Thus the Torah is a harmonious blend of positive and negative commandments, and a synthesis of the spiritual and physical elements of Creation. During this time period, we were also given the *mitzvos*, commandments to follow G-d's ways.

The Fourth Day of Creation was *Netzach,* victory and endurance. This was the day G-d created two luminaries in the sky, the sun and the moon. It was this millennium in which the two Holy Temples were built. The First Holy Temple was spiritually greater—and thus likened to the sun. The Second Temple, which is compared to the moon, radiated a dimmer light. Furthermore, the *Talmud*[11] states that *Netzach* is associated with Jerusalem, the city of our destiny, our faith, and our ultimate Redemption.

The Fifth Day of Creation was *Hod. Hod* means acknowledgment. It can also denote devastation. This was the day G-d created "sea monsters" and the ocean began to swarm with creatures. Birds were also created on this day and they began to fly in the sky. The Fifth Millennium was a generation of massacres, expulsions, and horrific difficulties for the Jewish people. It states in the book of *Eichah* (Lamentations): "The entire day was devastating."[12] We must ultimately balance *Hod's* devastation, however, with the fact that throughout this era, the Jewish people passionately acknowledged G-d. The fifth "day" was the millennium when thousands of Jews, upon dying during the Crusades, cried out "*Shema Yisrael*—G-d is our L-rd, G-d is One." The Jewish people, even on the brink of annihilation, acknowledged their Creator.

---

11 *Berachos* 58a.
12 *Eichah* 1:13.

The Sixth Day of Creation was *Yesod,* which means both building a foundation and bonding. This was the day that Adam, the first man, the foundation of the human race, was created. G-d first fashioned the entire world and then brought man into it. From this we learn that it is man's obligation to form a connection or bond between the material and the spiritual realms by using every aspect of the physical world in the service of G-d.

Yesod also represents the Sixth Millennium. As explained in *Chassidus,* Adam is the prototype of *Mashiach,* who is the perfect man. The word "Adam" is spelled אדם. The *alef* (*gematria* one) represents intellect, the first of a person's ten faculties. *Dalet,* the second letter of Adam, is the first letter of *dibbur,* or speech. *Mem* signifies *maaseh,* action.[13] Thus Adam, or *Mashiach,* will be perfect in his thought, speech, and action. Furthermore, the *Or HaChaim*[14] writes[15] that the sparks of redemption first began to appear in the 500th year of the Sixth Millennium (the year 1740 on the Gregorian calendar). Given that the *Talmud*[16] has stated that "all the affixed times for *Mashiach's* arrival have already passed," it is up to us to increase in acts of goodness and kindness to usher in *Mashiach's* arrival now.

Meaning

While the design of the *vav* looks like a hook, the word *vav* actually means "hook."[17] A hook is something that holds two things together. It is also a means to connect the spiritual and the physical. As in the story above, "If a man is connected on high, he doesn't fall down below."

---

13 *Likkutei Torah, Parshas Behaalos'cha,* p. 31c. Also see *Likkutei Sichos,* vol. 16, p. 473.
14 Rabbi Chaim Ibn Attar (1696-1743).
15 On *Leviticus* 6:2 and *Numbers* 26:22.
16 *Sanhedrin* 97b.
17 See *Exodus* 26:32, where the word *vaveihem* means "hooks."

On a syntactic level, adding a *vav* to the beginning of any word creates the meaning "and"; for example, *v'eileh* means "*and* these things." Within a sentence, "and" is the hook that connects one word or clause to the next. Furthermore, the *vav* attached to a verb converts that verb from either the past to the future tense, or from the future to the past tense. For example, the word *hoiya* in Hebrew means "it was." The word *v'hoiya* means "it will be." By merely attaching the *vav*, the past is transformed into the future. In reverse, consider the word *yehi*, which means "it shall be," as in "*Yehi or*[18]—[And G-d said,] "Let there be light." Place a *vav* in front—*vayehi*—and the meaning becomes, "There *was* light," in the past tense.

With this in mind, we can appreciate a lesson from the Rebbe as stated in his commentary to the *Tanya*:[19] "In the Torah there are fifty-three portions. All except ten begin with a *vav*. Similarly the *Tanya*,[20] also known as the Written Law of Chassidic thought, has in its first section fifty-three chapters. All fifty-three, with the exception of ten, begin with a *vav*."

Why do ten chapters in both the Torah and *Tanya* not begin with the letter *vav*? Perhaps the answer is the following:

Torah is often compared to water.[21] Just as water courses down the steep mountains to the valley below without changing its life-giving essence, so does the Torah reach man in its original, essential form. Torah began in Heaven, emanating from G-d, and then traveled—and continuously travels—down to the physical world utterly intact.

This message is conveyed through the letter *vav*, which is a hook connecting the higher realm to the lower; the chute that allows Torah to flow to man. Historically, the Torah also con-

---

18 *Genesis* 1:3.
19 Introduction to *Reshimos* on *Tanya*.
20 Written by Rabbi Schneur Zalman of Liadi and first published in 1797. The *Tanya* has been reprinted approximately 4,600 times, in every major city around the world.
21 *Taanis* 7a; *Tanya*, ch. 4.

nects the laws and customs of the past to the present; and thus the present to the future. Like the *vav*, which has the ability to shift a word, phrase, or idea from past to future and back, the Torah is both within time and beyond time. Its timeless teachings bridge life at the beginning of Creation with the current issues of modern-day life.

One could say that the ten portions of Torah and the ten chapters of *Tanya* that do *not* begin with a *vav* draw attention to the Ten Commandments and the Ten Utterances (of speech) with which G-d created the world.[22]

As the *Zohar*[23] explains: "If a Jew follows the Ten Commandments of the Torah, the world which was created with the Ten Utterances will continue to exist. If, however, he does not, G-d forbid, then the world will revert to primordial chaos."

Thus the *vav* teaches us the monumental effect we have on the world by being connected on high and bringing the Torah down to earth in our thoughts, speech and actions.

---

22 *Ethics of Our Fathers* 5:1 states that the Ten Utterances: "Let there be light," "Let there be a firmament," etc., actually caused these things to be created. See introductory section of this book, in the section "Energy in the Letters."

23 III, 11b; see also *Shabbos* 88a.

זכור

Zayin

ZAYIN—SHABBOS, THE CROWN OF CREATION

Design	1. Sword 2. crown 3. scepter
Gematria	Seven
Meaning	1. Crown 2. weapon 3. sustain

Rabbi Jacob J. Hecht, o.b.m., my maternal grandfather, once told me the following story: In the times when the Jews lived in the *shtetl*–long before the New York Lottery came along– there would be a traveling lottery "agent" who would station himself every week in a different *shtetl* and sell tickets. In this one particular town everyone bought a ticket. Everyone, that is, besides Shlamazal. You all know what a *shlamazal* is: someone who has two left hands and two left feet–who can't do anything right. Shlamazal refused to buy a ticket. After a lot of arm twisting, the *shtetl* people convinced Shlamazal to buy a ticket, and he did. In those days you wrote your own number on the ticket and then you put the ticket in a communal hat. When the ticket was drawn, to everyone's surprise, the winner was... Shlamazal!

When asked how he won, he answered with a newfound intelligence: "Ah, it was very simple. Everyone *knows* that to win a lottery, you only need two things: brains and *mazal*. Now, my mother always told me that seven is a lucky num- ber. Seven reminds us of the Shabbos, the seventh and holiest day of the week. Seven reminds us of the seventh year called *Shemittah*, the Sabbatical year when the land lay fallow; also the *Hakhel* year–the year when all of Israel, men, women, and children, came to the Holy Temple to be inspired by the king–which took place once every seven years. So I used my brains. I said, 'If one times seven is good and holy, then seven times seven is even better and holier.' So for my number, I picked forty-eight." The people shouted, "But seven times seven is *forty-nine*!!" Shlamazal said, "Yeh, that's where the *mazal* comes in. I was never good in mathematics."

Design

The seventh letter of the *alef-beis* is *zayin*. Its design is the form of a sword. The top of the *zayin* is the handle, and the vertical leg is the blade. Another interpretation of the *zayin's* design is that it represents a crown and a scepter. The *zayin* thus alludes to power and authority.

Gematria

The numerical value of the letter *zayin* is seven. Seven represents the seventh day of the week, which is Shabbos. It is the day G-d rested. But what does this mean? If G-d is infinite, why did He have to rest? A human, a mortal, is tired after a hard week at work, so he has to take a breather. But G-d, the immortal Being?

The answer is that the rest is not for G-d but for us. Since we work for six days a week and appear to be the masters of our fate, we can easily come to believe that *we* are the ones who have the power to determine our success. Therefore G-d instructs, "On the seventh day you are to stop. You are to examine the world around you and understand that everything comes from Me." Shabbos is the day to focus on the Creator of the universe.

We also find that many of the foods we eat on Shabbos are connected to the number seven. After *shul* on Friday night and Shabbos day, *Kiddush* is made on wine. The Hebrew word for wine is *yayin,* spelled יין, *yud-yud-nun.* If one adds up the *gematria* of יין, it equals 70, or 7.[1] After *Kiddush,* everyone then washes and returns to the table to say the blessing on and eat *challah*–bread. The *gematria* of חלה, *challah,* is 43, and[2] 4 and 3=7. After they eat the *challah,* of course they have gefilte fish. The word "fish," דג (*dag*), is spelled *dalet*=4 and *gimmel*=3, equaling 7. After the gefilte fish they move on to the soup, which is מרק (*merak*): *mem*=40, *reish*=200, *kuf*=100. Together

---

1 According to the calculation known as *mispar katan* (the "small count") in which the zeros are dropped, seventy is considered as seven.
2 Using the *mispar katan.*

they equal 340, and 3 and 4=7. After the soup, they proceed to the meat. Meat is בשר (basar): beis=2, shin=300, reish=200, equaling 502—again seven. All of the foods are a delicious reminder that we are partaking of the seventh day, the holy Sabbath.

The sanctity of seven is not only true in the microcosm, but in the macrocosm as well. With the First Day of Creation representing the first thousand years of the world's existence, the Second Day representing the second thousand years, etc., Shabbos represents the Seventh Millennium, which is "a day of rest and tranquility for all eternity."[3]

As we are currently in the year 5763 from Creation,[4] we are now in the Sixth Millennium. To figure out what "time" we're inhabiting in that millennium, we need to make some calculations: One thousand years represents one day, or 24 hours of creation. One thousand divided by 24 is 41.67 years per universal hour. If we then divide 41.67 into 763 (the years left after removing the root 5,000, signifying the Sixth Millennium) we get 18.29. We are thus currently 18.29 hours (approximately 18 hours and 17 minutes) past the preceding sunset, and are in "Friday afternoon," at the cusp of Shabbos. We are living right on the edge of the Seventh Millennium, the eternal Shabbos, the "day" of eternal tranquility. And when do we begin preparing in earnest for Shabbos as well as for *Mashiach's* arrival? Whether by the clock or calendar, it's Friday at noon (12:00 noon/the year 5750)![5] Preparation for this era is not something we can scramble for at the very last minute. It is something we must build toward with intention and joy.

---

3 The end of Tractate *Tamid.*

4 Based on the publication date of this book.

5 See *Sefer HaSichos 5750*, p. 254, 256. In that *sicha*, the Rebbe also cites a second opinion that brings the year 5750 even closer to the onset of Shabbos. In this calculation, which divides the millennium by the twelve daylight hours (vs. twenty-four hours), the current year corresponds to 3:00 p.m. before Shabbos.

One of the things the Rebbe instructed us to do in this generation to prepare for *Mashiach* is to learn the concepts relating to the subject of *Mashiach*, especially how they are illuminated in the teachings of *Chassidus*. Although *Mashiach* will surely come by the year 6,000, the Rebbe tells us that his coming is imminent due to the collective *teshuvah* and good deeds we have done in the past two thousands years of this last exile.

Rabbi Chaim Vital[6] tells us that compared to the Torah of *Mashiach*, the revealed Torah that we learn now is *hevel*— nothing. As related in the chapter on *alef*, the Baal Shem Tov once went up to the chamber of *Mashiach* in heaven and asked, "*Mashiach*, when are you going to come? When are you going to liberate the Jews from this terrible dark exile?" *Mashiach* answered, "When the wellsprings of your teachings, [i.e., the teachings of *Chassidus*,] spread forth throughout the entire world. The entire world will begin to learn the secrets of the Torah. Then I will come."

The Alter Rebbe expounded upon the teachings of the Baal Shem Tov in his *Tanya*[7] and other writings, and this philosophy has been transmitted all the way down to the Rebbe, the seventh Rebbe of Chabad Lubavitch. Therefore, it is incumbent upon every Jew who "awaits the coming of *Mashiach*" to delve into these teachings.

One must not wait until he is a master of the entire *Talmud* before he begins studying these mystical insights. Just as the *Shulchan Aruch* (the *Code of Jewish Law*) tells us[8] that on Friday afternoon it is customary to take a taste from the foods of Shabbos, so, too, in *this* generation we should taste from the

6 A disciple of the holy *AriZal*, Rabbi Isaac Luria. All the written teachings of the *AriZal* in our possession today were transmitted by Rabbi Chaim Vital (1543-1620).

7 Rabbi Joseph B. Soloveitchik (1903-1993), head of Yeshiva University, once related, "If not for my Chabad *melamed* (Chassidic teacher), I would today be lacking in an entire *dimension* of knowledge... Even today, I still know sections of the *Tanya* by heart." From *The Rav*, by Rabbi Aaron Rakeffet-Rothkoff, vol. 1, p. 147, KTAV Publishing House, Inc., Jersey City, NJ, 1999.

8 *Shulchan Aruch of the Alter Rebbe*, vol. II, ch. 250:8.

Shabbos Millennium, where we will be preoccupied with study-ing the secrets of Torah. The way to "taste" this millennium is by studying the teachings of *Chassidus* and infusing the aura of *Mashiach* into our everyday activities.

The *Midrash*[9] tells us that when G-d first created the world, G-dliness was manifest in everyday, physical life. However, seven grave sins caused G-d to remove Himself seven levels from this world. The first sin was that of Adam in the Garden of Eden. After Adam, there was the sin of Cain, who murdered his brother. Then there was the sin of Enosh, who began to serve idols ... and so on until the seventh sin which completed G-d's retreat to the farthest heaven. Then came Abraham who reversed the trend. By teaching his generation about the one G-d, he brought G-d down from the seventh heaven to the sixth. The righteous acts of his son Isaac brought G-d down another level to the fifth. Jacob drew G-d down one more level... until finally, Moses (the seventh leader of Israel) brought G-d back down to earth, amongst us at Mount Sinai. After receiving the Ten Commandments, the Jewish people sinned with the Golden Calf. G-d then removed Himself from the present world and ascended back to the first heaven. This cycle of up and down, *mitzvos* versus sins, holiness versus evil, has repeated itself throughout history. In our current cycle, G-d's return to the world began with the Alter Rebbe. The Alter Rebbe brought G-d down from the seventh to the sixth level. The progression has continued to this current generation, which stands poised for the revelation of *Mashiach*. The Rebbe has repeatedly told us that our generation is the seventh generation since the Alter Rebbe,[10] and thus the generation of Redemption. Just as it was Moses' generation (the seventh) that left Egypt, so will our generation leave this *golus*, or exile.

9 See *Basi LeGani 5710*, ch. 1.
10 *Basi LeGani 5711*, ch. 3.

One may ask, why are *we* the ones who are so meritorious? Why is our generation the one that deserves to leave the exile? The answer is this: Shabbos, the holiest day of the week, is on the seventh day. *The seventh is beloved by G-d.*[11] It is not necessarily our individual qualities, but the mere fact that we *find* ourselves in this era that makes us the last generation of exile and the first generation of Redemption.

On Friday afternoon, at the eve of Shabbos, we begin to feel this aura, this special light and inspiration at the cusp of the era of *Mashiach*.

Meaning

The name *zayin* means "crown." There are actually crowns, called *zayenin*,[12] on many of the letters of the *alef-beis*.

The word *zayin* also means "weapons"—as in the phrase *k'lei zayin*[13] (and as mentioned, the *zayin* looks like a sword). In addition, *zayin* means *zun*, "to sustain." In essence, these three definitions are interrelated. Shabbos, the crown of Creation, is also the day that blesses and therefore sustains the following week. By observing Shabbos, one accesses these blessings, which then gives us the weapon to overcome all negativity, especially the *yetzer hara*, the evil inclination.

As stated previously, one of the things that tempts us during the work-week is our belief that it is our ability and efforts alone that shape and control our fate. This belief then opens the door to the evil inclination in all its facets. The crown and sword of Shabbos remind us that G-d and *only* G-d is the Master of our fate, and this belief gives us the ability to conquer

---

11 *Vayikra Rabbah* 29:9.
12 According to Jewish law, the following seven letters (known by the acronym *shatnez getz*) must be written with crowns: *shin, ayin, tes, nun, zayin, gimmel, tzaddik.* ץ״ג ז״טנטעש. *Shulchan Aruch of the Alter Rebbe,* vol. I, ch. 36:5.
13 See *Makkos* 10a.

all negative forces. Indeed, blessings are our truest, most reliable weapons.

The meanings of *zayin* also parallel the Seventh Millennium. When G-d created the world, He did not want a world of war and destruction, hate and envy, sickness and death. He could easily have created a perfect world, but desired, rather, that man have the merit of helping Him achieve that state. Knowing this gives us the power to sustain ourselves and bolster our faith during these last moments of exile, and overcome the darkness and difficulty we are experiencing.

When *Mashiach* comes, there will no longer be evil upon the earth—as it states: "...and the spirit of impurity will be removed from upon the earth."[14] Believing in *Mashiach* helps bring about the transformation spoken of by the prophet Isaiah in which: "They shall beat their swords into plowshares and their spears into pruning hooks. Nation shall not lift up sword against nation, neither shall they learn war any more."[15] All of this is contained in the letter *zayin*.

14 *Zechariah* 13:2.
15 *Isaiah* 2:4.

וזנובה

Ches

CHES—MARRIAGE

Design	Vav and zayin plus bridge
Gematria	Eight
Meaning	Life

Before marrying my grandmother, Rebbetzin Chava Hecht, my grandfather, Rabbi Jacob J. Hecht, o.b.m., told her, "I, being a 'Yanky,' an old-fashioned American boy, will marry you only under the following condition: I must be the *head* of the house." My grandmother responded, "You can be the head, but I will be the *neck*, and wherever the neck turns, the head has to follow."

Design

The eighth letter of the *alef-beis* is the *ches*. The *ches*, according to the *AriZal*,[1] is a fusion of two letters: the *vav* and the *zayin*. On top of the *vav* and *zayin* is a *chatoteres*,[2] a bridge that unites the two.[3] In essence, *vav* represents the male principle, the husband. *Zayin* represents the female principle, the wife.[4] The bridge that links them is G-d. The Maggid of Mezritch illuminates[5] the verse "The woman of valor is the crown of her husband"[6] as: the *zayin*, the crown, signifies the position of the woman of valor safeguarding the man.

The design of the *ches* is representative of another type of bridge. If the relationship between *vav* (man) and *zayin* (woman) is to be complete, the two are united beneath a *chuppah*, a marriage canopy. The form of the *ches* looks like a marriage canopy. The word *chuppah*, חופה, even begins with a *ches*, for the word *chuppah* means *ches po–ches* (G-d, man and woman) is *po* (here). *Ches* is the heart of marriage. Man and woman are

---

1 The saintly Rabbi Isaac Luria (1534-1572), foremost founder of *Kabbalistic* teachings.
2 Literally a "hump."
3 *Matzos Shmurim* 31a and *Mishnat Chassidim, Tikkun Tefillin* 1:9; *Shulchan Aruch of the Alter Rebbe*, vol. I, ch. 36:2.
4 The *vav*, designed as a downward chute, alludes to the benefactor or the male. The *gematria* of *zayin*, seven, alludes to Shabbos—the female—or recipient of the six previous days. As it states, one that prepares food before Shabbos eats on the Shabbos.
5 *Or Torah, Remez* 24.
6 *Mishlei* 12:4.

truly united only when they are joined beneath the *chuppah* with the third partner, which is G-d.

The *Talmud*[7] tells us that if man and woman, איש ואשה (*ish v'isha*), are meritorious, the Divine presence will rest between them. The word *ish*, man, is spelled איש, *alef, yud, shin*. Isha, אשה, woman, is spelled *alef, shin, hei*. In both *ish* and *isha* we find the letters *alef* and *shin*. *Alef* and *shin* spell *eish*, the Hebrew word for fire. The fire that exists between man and woman fuels a fiery, passionate relationship. But if there were *only* this flame igniting the marriage, the fire of passion could all too easily be transformed into a fire of destruction. G-d must also be in the marriage, and fortunately He is: the *yud* of the *ish*, the man, when combined with the *hei* of the *isha*, the woman, denotes the very name of G-d.[8]

The comparison of a husband and wife's relationship to fire illustrates the secret to a healthy marriage. When two people decide to marry, there is usually fire and passion. Yet for some reason, two or three years down the line, the excitement is often gone. No fire. Where did the passion go?

When a relationship begins, it is like a bonfire, and who needs to tend a bonfire? One believes that it will last forever. But in truth, the flame has to be stoked. For example, a husband can surprise his wife with flowers for Shabbos. A wife can buy her husband a gift. They can attend a class together or establish a time to learn a portion of the Torah every week. They can take long romantic walks.

Additionally, a fire cannot be sustained unless the couple works together toward a common goal. Collaborating on different projects can help bond husband and wife. For example, planning a nice Shabbos meal with lots of guests is a great way

---

7 *Sotah* 17a.

8 The last two letters of the Tetragrammaton, the *Vav* and the *Hei*, allude to the son and daughter that will soon be born (*Reishis Chochmah, Shaar HaKedushah*, ch. 13).

to bond. The important thing to remember is that one shouldn't expect a marriage to last by itself. Unfortunately, in the United States today, more than fifty percent of marriages end in divorce. The key to maintaining fire in a marriage is nurturing the kernels of communication and purpose. The two partners must work together to fortify the *chatoteres*, the bridge, which unites them and binds them both to G-d.

Gematria

The numerical value of *ches* is eight. On the eighth day after his birth, a boy has a *bris*. What does a *bris* have to do with marriage? Well, one can say that after marriage there will be children, hopefully, and therefore, a *bris*. But in essence, the number eight represents transcendence—a level beyond nature and intellect. Everything in the world of time revolves around the number seven: the seven days of the week, the seventh year being a Sabbatical year, the observance of a *Hakhel* year every seven years. Eight, however, represents transcendence, a level that is beyond the natural order.

To explain, the *Midrash*[9] tells us there was a debate between Isaac and Ishmael, the two sons of Abraham. Ishmael said, "I'm better than you. Why? Because I had my *bris* when I was thirteen years old. Therefore I went into it rationally. I thought about it, made my choice and did it. And I still remember it to this very day. You, on the other hand, Isaac, don't remember anything; you never had that choice. You didn't have the opportunity to agree to it. It was done by force, without your consent." Isaac looked at Ishmael in turn and said, "No, on the contrary. I'm the one who is better off, because I had my *bris* at eight days rather than at thirteen years."

9 *Bereishis Rabbah* 55:4.

What did Isaac mean?[10] The word *bris* means "covenant," a bond between two sides. If two cohorts like each other, they say, "*Now* we are treating each other nicely, we're friends. But what about the future? Let's sit down and make a pact to ensure that we'll be friends forever. Forever means that even though there may come a time when, perhaps logically, we should separate—maybe we're not getting along, or one of us is causing the other pain—this pact will keep us together."

This *bris* is the pact a Jew makes with G-d on the eighth day of his life. One can say to G-d, "I'm not perfect and I don't follow Your Torah to the letter of the law. But You are my G-d. Therefore You will protect me, You will sustain me, and You will watch over me." On the other hand, even if G-d doesn't treat us the way we think we should be treated, even if He allows us to be in *golus* (exile) one more moment, G-d forbid, we won't reject Him. We won't forsake Him, because we have a *bris*—a covenant beyond intellect—demanding that we stay together.

We can thus understand the advantage of a *bris* done on the eighth day versus one done at thirteen years. Even though a person has free will in the latter case, his choice is made on a rational level. In contrast, a *bris* that is performed on the eighth day represents one's bond with G-d that defies all levels of intellect and the natural order.

In much the same way, the Jewish people's marriage to G-d is also a relationship that transcends logic. It is a suprarational covenant, bonding both parties for eternity.

Meaning

The meaning of the word *ches* is *chayos*, which means "life." Life can only be considered true when it is infused with G-dliness, because the body by itself is temporary, and anything

---

10 *Likkutei Sichos*, vol. 25, p. 86ff.

temporary cannot be true. True life is immortal and everlasting. The way one acquires everlasting life is by connecting with G-d through Torah study and the performance of *mitzvos*.

In addition, the *Zohar*[11] tells us that before an individual gets married, he is only "half a person." It is only when he unites with his *bashert* (soulmate) in marriage that he becomes whole and complete. Since marriage allows one to connect to G-d in the ultimate sense, then being united with one's soulmate is considered "true life."

Furthermore, the *AriZal* expounds on this idea of completeness in terms of the specific *mitzvos* that a woman is not obligated to perform,[12] explaining that she indeed receives the merit of the *mitzvah* when it is performed by her soulmate.[13] Soulmates are partners in this regard; even before their marriage.

Because certain *mitzvos* can only be done within the context of marriage, this process of shared merit is not considered complete until the two halves of the soul unite under the *chuppah*. G-d's participation in the marriage is the *chatoteres*, the bridge, which brings the union to fruition and creates everlasting *chayos*.

The *Talmud* states:[14] "It is as difficult for G-d to make a match between two people as the Splitting of the Red Sea." Obviously, this statement raises a few questions. What does the Red Sea have to do with marriage? And how can we call something that G-d accomplishes "difficult"? G-d is omnipotent,

---

11 III, p. 7b, 109b, 296a.

12 *Taamei HaMitzvos, Bereishis, Shaar Maamarei Rashbi* on the *Tikkunei Zohar 469.* See also *Likkutei Sichos,* vol. 31, p. 96ff.

13 For example, when a woman's husband puts on *tefillin* (or any *mitzvah* that she is not required to perform), she gets the spiritual benefit of his observance of the *mitzvah*.

On the other hand, if both parties are equally obligated in a *mitzvah*, one's performance does not exempt the other's obligation. An example would be eating matzah on Pesach, which is a commandment for both men and women. If the husband eats matzah on Pesach, the wife is still obligated to do so herself. And if the husband eats matzah but she eats bread, she has transgressed the commandment regardless of his actions.

14 *Sotah* 2a.

infinite. Yet we say that His bringing about a marriage is as difficult as the Splitting of the Red Sea! Furthermore, if one wanted to talk about something being difficult, why pick the Red Sea? In the grand scheme of things, why not mention something even more intimidating—like the creation of the universe?!

The answer is as follows. When G-d created the world, He formed it ex nihilo—from nothing into something. If a contractor is given the job of building a house from scratch, it is relatively easy. There are no standing walls to bother him and no limits to constrain him. He is able to do what he wants to create the perfect home. But what happens when an individual moves into a home that is dilapidated? What if the walls are crooked and he has to straighten them out? What if the pre-existing plumbing is a shambles? It is a lot harder to make that structure into a perfect home. We find a direct parallel in the Splitting of the Red Sea. The nature of water is to flow. But what did G-d do at the Sea? He took the fluid nature of water and transformed it into the nature of solid rock.[15] He had to completely change the substance from its elemental norm. The same is true of marriage. There are two different people who come from two different homes with two different backgrounds. It is not challenging enough that one is a male and one is a female. Beyond that, *he* likes the windows open; she likes the windows closed. He likes the country. She likes the city. His mother made gefilte fish *this* way. Her mother made gefilte fish *that* way. So we have these two opposites coming together and trying to merge as one. In order for the marriage to work, the nature and constitution of each individual must change.

Now we can understand why it is as difficult for G-d to create a marriage as it is to split the Red Sea, because in order for two people to come together, each must change his or her ingrained

15 See *Tanya, Shaar HaYichud VehaEmunah*, ch. 2, for a more detailed discussion.

habits and ways. In order for a marriage to survive, and better yet, thrive, there needs to be a third element, a third partner, G-d, who helps the two natures to fuse.

At the Splitting of the Sea, G-d blew a wind all night long to keep the water standing. Why? Because if we are going to transform the very nature of something, we must continuously infuse that element with new life, breath and force. Therefore a marriage—which requires constant change by the two individuals involved—must be continuously infused with the spirit of G-d. This is the true *ches*, the true *chayos*: man, woman and G-d coming together in the eternal covenant of marriage.

ט

טאַנץ

_____

Tes

_____

TES—THIS TOO IS FOR THE BEST

Design	1. Vessel (with bent lid) 2. bending one's head in prayer
Gematria	Nine
Meaning	Good or best

Avraham Rothenberg, an Israeli descendant of the Rabbinic dynasty of Gerer chassidim, had been a teacher in Brazil for five years. On one of his trips back to Israel, he stopped off in New York, visited Chabad, and was very impressed. He eventually moved to Crown Heights, Brooklyn.

One night, the loud ringing of the telephone woke him from his sleep. His brother was calling from Israel with very troubling news: their father had suffered a serious heart attack a few hours before. His condition was serious, almost critical.

As soon as Avraham put down the receiver, he considered immediately booking a flight to Israel, but on second thought he realized that his traveling could not help the situation. Instead, he decided to write a letter to the Rebbe, asking for his holy blessing.

Fearing the worst, he began to write with a trembling hand. It was extremely difficult for him to concentrate. His mind would not let him rest. "I don't know what to think," were the final words in his letter.

With a heavy heart, he handed the letter to the Rebbe's secretary. While he was waiting for an answer, he took out his Book of Psalms and began to recite some chapters. The tears choked him... *Creator of the Universe... Why?!*

A few minutes later, the Rebbe's secretary handed him back the letter he had written. The Rebbe had struck a line through the words "I don't know what to think," and wrote the following in the margin:

"Amazing. The command of our Sages in such situations is well known: *Tracht gut, vet zain gut* ("Think positively and it will be good"), and I expect to hear good news."

Instantaneously, Avraham's mood changed from one extreme to another. He was filled with optimism and hope for a better future for his father, as if someone had shaken him out of his lethargy, out of those destructive thoughts that had brought him to depression. The color returned to his face. He opened his Book of Psalms with renewed faith in G-d. The words flowed from his mouth with joy. His trust in the Rebbe and in the Rebbe's instructions to think positively put hope for immediate salvation in his heart.

He went to phone his family in Israel for the latest news about his father. The news was encouraging: "Father's condition is no longer listed as life-threatening."

But the big surprise came a few days later, after the *Minchah* service, when he met the Rebbe on his way out of the *beis midrash*. "*Nu*, do you have any good news for me?" the Rebbe asked him.

"Yes, I spoke with my family on the phone, and my father's condition has improved."

"When did this happen?" the Rebbe questioned.

"Two days ago."

"And when did you begin to 'think positively'?"

"As soon as I received the Rebbe's response, two days ago."

"You see," the Rebbe said. "Even though you should never have to know from such things, be aware that one should always 'think positively.'"

Avraham Rothenberg's father merited seventeen more years of life. (The *gematria* of the word *tov*, טוב, (good) is seventeen.) He was even able to travel to the United States to meet the Rebbe himself.[1]

Design

Tes is the ninth letter of the *alef-beis*.

---

[1] From *Wonders and Miracles*, published by *Maareches Ufaratzta*, Kfar Chabad, Israel, 1993, p. 190.

The design of the *tes* is like a pot, a vessel with an inverted rim, representing hidden or inverted good.[2] Another interpretation of the *tes* is that it represents a man bending his head to G-d in prayer and thanks.[3] How are the two connected? We just explained the letter *ches* as representing the concept of marriage. After the union between husband and wife, then, G-d willing, there's a conception. The *tes* represents the hidden good that resides within the womb (the vessel) of the mother. This hidden good is actualized through a person's prayers to G-d, asking Him for a healthy child.

Gematria

The numerical value of *tes* is nine. This corresponds to the nine months of pregnancy. Furthermore, the number nine is a "true" number. Truth or אמת (*emes*), is spelled *alef*—the first letter of the *alef-beis*; *mem*—the middle letter; and the *tav*[4]—the last letter. The lesson is that something that is true must be true at the beginning, middle, and end.

What makes nine a "true" number is that if you multiply any whole number by nine, the sum of its digits is also nine; e.g., two times nine is eighteen; one plus eight is nine. Three times nine is twenty-seven; two plus seven is nine. Nine times nine is eighty-one; eight plus one is nine. Finally, the *gematria* of *emes* is 441: *alef*=1, *mem*=40, *tav*=400. 4 and 4 and 1=9. Nine represents the number of truth.

Meaning

The meaning of *tes* is *tov*, which means "good" or "best." A story is told in the *Talmud*[5] about the great Torah Sage Nachum Ish Gamzu who always said, "*Gam zu letovah*—This too is for

2 *The Alef-Beit, op. cit.*, p. 140.
3 *The Wisdom in the Hebrew Alphabet, op. cit.*, p. 123.
4 Or *sav* depending on the pronunciation of the letter.
5 *Taanis* 21a.

the best." One day, Nachum Ish Gamzu traveled to the Roman Emperor to give him a treasure chest full of precious metals and jewels as a gift on behalf of his community. That night he slept at an inn and stowed the jewel-laden chest in a secret hiding place. When Nachum Ish Gamzu was asleep, the innkeeper switched the chest with another.

The next morning, when Nachum Ish Gamzu was about to leave the inn, he opened the chest, and to his dismay there were no longer diamonds and rubies inside. Instead, the entire vessel was filled with sand. Nachum Ish Gamzu said, "*Gam zu letovah*—This too is for the best," and continued on his way. He arrived at the palace and said, "Emperor, because of our great respect for you, my town is presenting this gift to you." The Emperor opened the chest and saw the sand. He thought, well, there must be something else beneath it. He sifted through the sand. He dug his hand into one side of the chest, then the other. But all he found was sand. The Emperor said, "For mocking me, I will have you put to death." Nachum Ish Gamzu's reaction was, of course, "*Gam zu letovah.*" Immediately, in walked one of the sovereign's advisers (the *Talmud* tells us it was Elijah the Prophet in the guise of a Roman senator). "What are you talking about?" Elijah declared. "Do you think the Jews are so stupid? Do you think they are so foolish they'd give you simple sand?! This must be the same sand that Abraham (the Patriarch) used when he fought against the four kings.[6] Abraham single-handedly conquered the most powerful kings of his time. Do you know how he did it? He possessed magic sand. He threw it into the air and the sand turned into knives and spears and arrows."

"Really?" responded the Emperor. "Let's try it out."

At that time, the Emperor's forces were in the midst of a war. They were trying to conquer a neighboring province, so the

6 *Midrash Tanchuma* on *Genesis* 14.

Emperor sent this chest to the front lines with his soldiers and they began to throw handfuls of sand toward the enemy. Lo and behold, the sand was transformed into these magic secret weapons! In a day or two, the Roman army was able to overwhelm the entire province. The Emperor thanked Nachum Ish Gamzu, saying, "Because you did this for me, I'm going to reward you with a chest of gold and silver. Take it back to your people and tell them that if they should ever need anything, they should come to me. I'll be happy to oblige them."

On his way back home, Nachum Ish Gamzu stopped at the same inn. The proprietor asked him, "What gift did you bring the Emperor that he showed you such honor?" He replied, "Well, you know, I had this chest full of sand. I brought it to the Emperor and this magical sand turned into arrows and spears when thrown at his enemies." The innkeeper heard this and said to himself, "Wow! That's the sand in my backyard!" So what did the man do? He filled up an entire wagon full of sand. The innkeeper brought it to the Emperor and said, "You know that sand Nachum Ish Gamzu brought you last week? This is the same stuff." The Emperor was overjoyed and immediately sent the wagon of sand to the troops. When the "magic sand" turned out to be a sham, the infuriated Emperor ordered the execution of this deceitful innkeeper.

There's a second famous story from the *Talmud*,[7] this one featuring Rabbi Akiva. Rabbi Akiva, a student of Nachum Ish Gamzu, would say, "*Kal d'avid Rachmana letav avid*–Whatever G-d does, must be for the good." The tale is told of how Rabbi Akiva traveled with a candle, a rooster, and a donkey: the candle so he could study Torah at night, the rooster–his alarm clock–to wake him up to study Torah, and finally the donkey to carry his possessions. Rabbi Akiva stopped at a city. He tried to get lodging at an inn but there was no room available. Rabbi

7 *Berachos* 60b.

Akiva went from house to house but nobody would let him in. So what did he do? He walked into the neighboring woods and set up camp. All of a sudden, a strong wind kicked up and extinguished the candle. A few moments later, a ferocious lion emerged from behind his tent and killed his donkey. What was left? The rooster. A ravenous cat appeared and devoured it. Rabbi Akiva was completely stuck. What did he say? "Whatever G-d does, must be for the good."

The next morning, Rabbi Akiva discovered that a band of robbers had attacked the town during the night, mercilessly killing the people and stealing their money. The robbers escaped into the forest. If they had seen the candle, or heard the noise of the rooster and donkey, Rabbi Akiva would have met the same fate as the townspeople. G-d had saved his life by extinguishing his candle and taking his animals.

Now, there's a big difference between the terminology of Nachum Ish Gamzu and that of Rabbi Akiva.[8] Nachum Ish Gamzu said, "*Gam zu letovah*": Even though something may appear negative, it is *itself* good. The chestful of sand itself was good, regardless of the loss of the precious jewels. And so it was. This was his philosophy, his ethos of living. Nachum Ish Gamzu's approach was not that he would *later* see the value of the sand; its worth was immediate and intrinsic.

On the other hand, in the story of Rabbi Akiva, the actual loss of his donkey and rooster, according to him, was *not* good. But it was a smaller loss compared to a greater loss. Rabbi Akiva would eventually see the good the very next day. But the immediate sacrifice was viewed as negative.

All of us can learn a practical lesson from the above. When we're taking a trip, for example, our tire might suddenly blow out. We think, "*Oy vey!* It's going to kill our plans. We'll have to spend hours changing the tire. Then we'll have to stay at a

8 *Likkutei Sichos*, vol. 2, p. 393ff.

motel instead of making the trip in one day." Now, we could say, "Perhaps G-d is saving us from yet a worse situation that would have taken place had we continued our trip as planned." But the *emes*—the truth—is that standing on the side of the road with a flat tire at that time is in *itself* good. Even events that are not readily perceived as being positive are totally good, since everything comes from G-d and G-d is all good.

This is the lesson of the *tes*.

Yud

YUD—AND THE TENTH SHALL BE HOLY

Design	1. Point 2. flame
Gematria	Ten
Meaning	1. Jew 2. hand (of G-d)
	3. continuity—Yehudah

As a young pupil, the Chassidic master, Reb Yisrael of Ruzhin,[1] was instructed by his teacher that whenever he saw two dots next to each other he was to pronounce G-d's name.[2] Now, at the end of a verse in the Torah, there are also two dots: one above the other. That evening at home, the young Reb Yisrael began to read. And every time he reached the end of a verse he uttered G-d's name. His father reprimanded him: "What's going on here?! Who taught you that?!" The boy responded, "My teacher did. He taught me that whenever I see two dots together, I should pronounce G-d's name. So that's what I'm doing."

Reb Yisrael's father explained to his son: "The dot, the *yud*, represents a Jew. When one Jew is beside another, when one Jew respects the other, then G-d dwells in their presence. Their alliance becomes G-d's name. But when one Jew is on top of the other, when one Jew thinks he's better or smarter than the next, or disrespects his neighbor, then that's the end of the passage. It creates a separation in the relation between a Jew and G-d.

Design

The tenth letter of the *alef-beis*—and also the smallest—is the letter *yud*.

On the simplest level, the design of the *yud* is a point: a dot which represents G-d's essential power; the one G-d Who is indivisible. Furthermore, the *yud* looks like a flame that soars ever higher, representing the soul of a Jew yearning to unite with G-d.[3]

Additionally, the *yud* represents the method by which the blessing descends from G-d to His people. The letter *yud* when

---

1 1796-1850.
2 Two "dots" or *yuds*, written *Yud-Yud*, represent two of G-d's holy names. See section on "Meaning" in this chapter.
3 *Tanya*, beginning of ch. 19.

spelled out is י-ו-ד. The *yud* represents a seminal drop, the concentrated power of G-d. The *vav* represents a descent, for its form is that of a chute—and through this the blessings of G-d travel downward to our world. The *dalet*, having height and width, represents the physical world, signifying how G-d's blessings are manifest in every aspect of nature. This teaches us that G-d's blessings don't only reside in heaven. They flow down to this corporeal world and endow us with physical health, sustenance and success.

Perhaps this is why the first letter of each of the three passages of the Priestly Blessing begins with the *yud:*[4]

יברכך ה׳ וישמרך—May G-d bless you and guard you.

יאר ה׳ פניו אליך ויחנך—May G-d shine His countenance upon you and be gracious to you.

ישא ה׳ פניו אליך וישם לך שלום—May G-d turn His countenance toward you and grant you peace.

Furthermore, every letter of the *alef-beis* begins with the *yud*, a point. This illustrates the inherent spirituality of every letter of the Hebrew alphabet, and that the Torah and G-d's teachings are all for the sake of the *Yid*, or Jew.

Gematria

The numerical equivalent of the *yud* is ten. Up until now, we've been discussing the single integers of the *alef-beis*. Now we enter the realm of two-digit numbers. After the *yud*, each letter's *gematria* increases by ten instead of one. *Yud* is ten, *kaf* is twenty, *lamed* is thirty, *mem* forty, and so on. In Judaism, the number ten is quite significant. Throughout the teachings of Torah, *Talmud*, *Kabbalah* and *Chassidus*, the number ten is a fundamental building block for every aspect of Creation.

Firstly, there are the Ten Utterances of Speech through which G-d created the world. Next come the ten generations from

4 *Zohar III*, 290b.

Adam to Noah, and the ten generations from Noah to Abraham. There were ten plagues that G-d brought upon the Egyptian people, and ten miracles that He performed for His people to save them from those plagues. G-d challenged the Jewish people with ten tests in the desert. And, of course, G-d gave us the Ten Commandments.[5]

The fact that ten represents sanctity and holiness is another reason for the importance of the *yud*. The *Talmud* tells us[6] that when ten Jews assemble, G-d dwells in their presence. The *Tanya*[7] gives an example of just how powerful that congregation is. It states that if an angel were to fly above the room in which ten Jews were gathered—even if there were no words of Torah exchanged between them—the angel would be burnt out of existence from the holy light that radiated from their combined energy. This is the power of ten souls. And if these ten souls are gathered together for Torah study and prayer, how much mightier is their force.

How do we know about the sanctity of ten? From the story of the *Meraglim*—the Spies. Moses sent twelve spies to scout the land of Canaan (the land of Israel). Two of the spies, Joshua and Caleb, delivered a positive report: "If G-d desires it... we shall surely ascend and conquer it."[8] The other ten reported negatively: "We cannot go up against those people.... It is a land that devours its inhabitants."[9] G-d responded, "How much longer must I remain amongst this evil congregation (*eidah*)?"[10] referring obviously to these ten men.

From here we learn that a congregation (an *eidah*) refers to a group of ten, a *minyan*. A number of important questions

5 *Ethics of Our Fathers*, ch. 5.
6 *Megillah* 23b.
7 *Tanya, Iggeres HaKodesh*, ch. 23.
8 *Numbers* 14:8; 13:30.
9 *Ibid.* 13:31-32.
10 *Ibid.* 14:27.

logically follow. Why is the concept of ten men constituting a *minyan* based on the fact that there were ten evil spies returning from the land of Israel? How do we ultimately say that ten traitors represent proof that G-d can only dwell among a community of at least ten, and that the *Shechinah* (a manifestation of G-dliness) can exist only in such a gathering?

In examining the treason of the Spies, we come to realize that, in essence, they weren't such grave sinners. The Spies were the heads of ten of the twelve Tribes. They were holy people.[11] When Moses sent them into the land of Israel, they saw a beautiful land, rich soil, a wonderful climate, and large, succulent fruits. Upon their return, they said to Moses, "It is a land that devours its inhabitants"—meaning—"It's not that we couldn't conquer Canaan's inhabitants physically, but if we reside in this materialistic environment, there is no way we would be able to maintain our current spiritual level. We will be swallowed up by materialism."

G-d chose us to study His holy Torah. He chose us to be a light unto all the nations of the world. How could the Jewish people accomplish this if, by living in Israel, by indulging in this physical wonderland, they would forget about their responsibilities? Instead of studying and praying all day they would be working the soil. They would be reaping delicious produce. And they would forget all about why they ultimately came. In the desert, the Jewish people were essentially provided for. They had manna from Heaven to eat. They had water from the well of Miriam to drink. Their clothes were washed and maintained by the Clouds of Glory. So what did they do all day? They learned Torah. They discussed its instructions and delved into its secrets.

In the *Rambam's Introduction to the Mishnah*, he discusses how the Oral Law was imparted to the people. Each time G-d

11 *Likkutei Torah*, beginning of *Shelach*; *Likkutei Sichos*, vol. 4, p. 1042; vol. 33, p. 86.

gave a law to Moses, Moses taught it four times: first to Aaron, then to Aaron's sons, then the seventy elders, and then the Jewish people.... After all this, the nation divided into small groups and discussed the particular law, analyzing it over and over again until they were utterly clear about every one of its aspects. This was the daily routine of the Jewish people in the desert.

Moses' spies were great Torah scholars and holy Jews. They said, "Look, if we go into the land of Israel, we're not going to have time to sit around and discuss all the minute details of *halachah*. We won't have the opportunity to analyze the law in depth, or pass it on scrupulously to our children. For *this* reason, Israel is a land that will eat up its inhabitants. The Jewish people will become immersed in the physical rather than the spiritual." The Spies therefore told Moses, "We don't want to go." Obviously this was a sin, but why was this a sin for which they were mortally punished? Because G-d's original and fundamental intention in bringing us into the world was *not* to eschew physicality, but to transform the physical into the spiritual. *That* is the ultimate goal of the Jewish nation.

So the incident of the Spies represents a rather unique paradox. The Spies sinned because they didn't follow G-d's objective in conquering the land. On the other hand, they had a valid point. They knew of the temptations that awaited the Jewish people.

Now imagine this scenario. A mother wakes up her eight-year-old son for school and he says, "No! I don't want to go and I'm not going to go!" How does the mother respond? Does she say, "Get up! You're going to school whether you like it or not"—or—"Oh, you don't want to go to school? No problem. But you'll have to stay in bed for the next forty years!" Obviously she'll tell him to go to school.

Similarly, when the Spies said, "We don't want to go into the land," why didn't G-d just ignore them and demand that they go in anyway?

Because they weren't ready. There was much more studying to be done.[12]

Now if *only* we would all be on the Spies' level—committed to learning Torah and striving to be spiritual and connected to G-d every minute of the day! In their own way, the Spies wanted the era of *Mashiach* to begin at that very moment.[13] But the time simply wasn't right. First, the Jewish people had to enter the Land. They had to work it and bring its fruits up to G-d, exemplifying how everything in this physical world is linked to the spiritual. Then and only then—in that era and our own—would we be fit for the coming of *Mashiach*. This is the richness of the passage from which we derive the concept of a *minyan*. To this very day, any time ten Jews gather for any reason it is a quorum of holiness.

Meaning

The meaning of *yud* is a *Yid*—a Jew. The *yud* can also represent a *yad*—a hand, which is an allusion to G-d, for we say that G-d took us out of Egypt with a mighty hand.

How do we differentiate between the *yud* that represents G-d and the *yud* that alludes to man? We see many times in our prayer books that the name of G-d is composed of two consecutive *yud*s, one immediately adjacent to the other. The two *yud*s constitute a vital force in two of G-d's names: The first name of G-d, the Tetragrammaton, is spelled ה-ו-ה-י—*Yud-Hei-Vav-Hei.* The Tetragrammaton represents G-d as He is *beyond* nature. The second name of G-d is *A-donai*—which is י-נ-ד-א—*Alef-Dalet-Nun-Yud.* It signifies how G-d, the Master of the universe,

---

12 *Likkutei Sichos,* vol. 33, p. 87.
13 See *Sefer HaSichos 5749,* vol. 2, p. 548, fn. 79; p. 549, fn. 87.

manifests Himself *in* nature. The *Yud* at the beginning of the Tetragrammaton and the *Yud* at the end of *A-donai* come together—a *Yud* followed by another *Yud*—to represent a fusion of these two expressions of G-dliness.[14] This fusion is an affirmation of the fact that while we live in a physical world of "natural" order, G-d is truly the one and only creator of nature.

The *yud* is also the first letter in the two names for a Jew. The first name is ישראל (*Yisrael*). Jews are called *b'nei Yisrael*—the children of Israel. *Yisrael* means both ראש לי[15]—"I am the head,"[16] and שר א-ל—"minister of G-d."[17] The terminology "minister of G-d" represents the spiritual aspect of a Jew when he prays, studies Torah, performs acts of loving-kindness and all the other *mitzvos*.

The second name for a Jew is *b'nei Yaakov*—the children of Jacob. *Yaakov* is a phonetic fusion of the letter *yud* and the word *akeiv*. *Yud* represents G-d. *Akeiv* means "heel," the lowest part of man. The heel is what we use to tread upon the earth. Therefore, the mission of a Jew is to go forth into the depths of the materialistic world and infuse it with the *Yud* of G-d, with G-dliness. This isn't true only with regard to the land of Israel or the synagogue. It refers to *every* place a Jew's foot lands. We must journey from Shabbos into the weekday and from prayer into business with the same intention, with the same passion to fulfill and complete G-d's creation.

We've just said that there are two names for a Jew. But from where does the *word* "Jew" (*Yehudi* in Hebrew) actually derive? We don't even see the term *Yehudi* in our texts until *Megillas Esther*, the scroll that we read on Purim.

In *Megillas Esther*, Mordechai refused to bow down to the wicked Haman. It says: "A man, a Jew (*ish Yehudi*), was in

---

14 *Ibid.*, p. 668 (a talk by the Rebbe in regard to the *shloshim* of Rabbi Jacob J. Hecht, o.b.m.).

15 Derived by switching the letters of the word *Yisrael*.

16 *Torah Or*, p. 50a, explained there to mean a person's G-dly soul.

17 *Likkutei Torah, Devarim*, p. 32b.

Shushan the capital, and his name was Mordechai."[18] The *Talmud*[19] observes that Mordechai didn't come from the tribe of Judah (Yehudah). Rather he belonged to the tribe of Benjamin. He should thus have been called "Mordechai the Benjaminite (*Yemini*)." The *Talmud* proceeds to state that anyone who denies idolatry and thereby acknowledges G-d is called a *Yehudi*— Yehudah, or the Jew.

It is interesting to note that the letter *yud*, when placed at the beginning of a word, represents constancy. This concept is illustrated in the verse in *Job*[20]: "So did Job do (*yaaseh*) all of his days." The verb *asah* (עשה), "to do," would typically refer to a one-time accomplishment. Here, however, a *yud* precedes it— יעשה. The *yud* empowers *asa* with continuity. Job offered burnt offerings for his children not just this one time, but every year at that time—all of his days.

The same concept holds true with G-d's name. The name of G-d is spelled *Yud-Hei-Vav-Hei*. The word *hoveh* (*hei, vav, hei*) means "the present." G-d continuously creates the world—right now, even as you read this. The *Yud* in front of *hoveh* reminds us that Creation was not a singular occurrence. Rather, G-d is forming the world anew every moment.[21]

The word Yehudah (i.e., *Yehudi*)—the Jew—also begins with a *yud*. The Alter Rebbe explains[22] that Yehudah means "praise" and "acknowledgment" (etymologically, it stems from the word *hod*, to praise). A Jew, by nature, praises G-d. But this isn't merely enacted once or twice in a lifetime, or even once or twice a day. Praise is expressed every moment of our earthly existence. This is the *yud* that is placed before the root word *hod*, "to praise." It represents a Jew's continuous, innate desire

18　*Esther* 2:5.
19　*Megillah* 13a.
20　Ch. 1:5.
21　*Tanya, Shaar HaYichud VehaEmunah*, ch. 4.
22　*Torah Or*, p. 45a.

to praise G-d. Of course, some days that desire can be concealed and we may be unaware of it. But that can never obscure a Jew's perpetual, unyielding connection to G-d.

In light of this fact, we may re-examine one of the darkest periods of Jewish history. Hitler—may his name be erased—forced all Jews to wear a yellow star with the word "Jude" (i.e., *Yehudi*) on it. In retrospect, we can say that Hitler's attempt to extinguish the Jewish spark actually served to re-ignite and distinguish it. Wearing the star meant that even in the most harrowing times, the Jewish people would never stop loving and praising G-d. Yehudah—*to praise G-d constantly*—was emblazoned on our very being.

Yud. G-d's indivisible power. His hand. His name. A corridor to a heightened level of connection and understanding—forever embedded in our Jewish name and our inherent desire to praise Him.

כך

כפרה שלג׳ען

_____

Kaf

KAF—KINGSHIP

Design	1. Bent pipe 2. submission to G-d
	3. the King of kings
Gematria	Twenty
Meaning	Crown

A king once traveled to a great forest. He penetrated so deeply into the forest that he got lost and could not find the way home. In the depths of the woods he met simple peasants and asked them to lead him out of the forest, but they were unable to help him, for they had never heard of the great highway that led to the royal palace.

The king then found a wise and understanding man, and requested his aid. The sage discerned immediately that this was the king and his heart stirred within him. In his wisdom, he immediately led the king to the correct path, guided him to his royal palace and aided him until the king was finally restored his true honor and seated on his majestic throne. The rescuer, of course, found great favor with the king.

Time passed and the wise man acted improperly, angering the king. The king ordered that he be tried for violating the royal law. The man knew that he would be dealt with very severely. In great anxiety, he fell before the king and implored that he be granted one plea: before the trial and the subsequent judgment, he wished to be garbed in the very same clothing he had worn when the king first encountered him in the forest. The king, too, was to don the original clothing he had been wearing then.

The king acceded to this request. When the forest encounter was re-enacted by their dressing in the original garments, the king vividly remembered the life-saving kindness of his rescuer. Great mercy was aroused within him as he recollected how he had been restored to the royal throne. With compassion and mercy, the king magnanimously forgave his rescuer and restored him to his place of high honor.

This story, told by Reb Levi Yitzchak of Berditchev,[1] is an analogy of the relationship between G-d and the Jewish people. Before the great revelation at Sinai, G-d went from nation to nation and offered them the Torah, but they declined it. We, the Jewish people, accepted the Torah with gladness and joy, affirming that "We will do and we will hear,"[2] accepting the Torah even prior to hearing its specific teachings. We declared our loyalty to G-d, "accepting the yoke of the Heavenly kingdom," proclaimed G-d's majesty as King over us, and affirmed that we would fulfill His commands and be loyal to His holy Torah.

Throughout our history, the Jewish people have sinned and rebelled against G-d... and every Rosh Hashanah we blow the *shofar*, reminiscent of the *shofar* that blew at Mount Sinai when we received the Torah. This reminds us of our vow to submit to G-d's sovereignty and evokes our thoughts of repentance. Through the *shofar* blowing, G-d remembers our original acceptance of the Torah when we made Him our King. He thus forgives us for all our sins and inscribes us immediately to the Book of Life for a good life, etc.[3] The *kaf*, the representation of *Kesser*, the crown of the King, reminds us that our intention in performing *mitzvos* must focus on our submission to G-d's will.[4]

Design

The eleventh letter of the *alef-beis* is the *kaf*.[5]

The design of the *kaf* can perhaps be described as a pipe bent in two places. The concept of bending oneself represents sub-

---

1 (1740-1809) A disciple of the Maggid of Mezritch and a contemporary of the Alter Rebbe. See *Kedushas Levi, Discourse on Rosh Hashanah*, p. 96. Also see *Likkutei Sichos*, vol. 34, p. 184.

2 *Exodus* 24:7.

3 *Tanya*, ch. 4.

4 *Ibid., Iggeres HaKodesh*, Epistle 29.

5 The *kaf* is sometimes pronounced *chaf*, depending primarily on its placement within a word.

mission to a greater force and entity—the King of all kings, A-lmighty G-d.

Gematria

The *gematria* of *kaf* is twenty. Twenty can be divided into ten and ten. The first ten represents the Ten Utterances with which G-d created the world. The second ten represents the Ten Commandments.[6] Together, they become a *kaf.* In *Numbers*[7] it states: "Ten-ten is the *kaf.*"[8]

If you take the word עשרים (*esrim,* the word "twenty" in Hebrew) and add up its letters, you arrive at 620: *ayin*=70, *shin*=300, *reish*=200, *yud*=10, *mem*=40. 620 is also the *gematria* of the word כתר, *kesser*: *kaf*=20, *tav*=400, *reish*=200. *Kesser* means crown, the ornament placed on the head of a king. *Kesser* also reminds us of the 620 letters in the Ten Commandments. G-d crowned the Jewish nation by giving them the Torah. And it became the Jews' *raison d'être* to follow the 613 commandments and the 7 Rabbinic laws[9]—which together total 620. Significantly, the first letter of *kesser* is *kaf.*[10]

In *Kabbalah,* the *Sefirah* (or faculty) of *Kesser* represents a level that is beyond intellect. The crown is placed atop the head. Of course, our head is the vessel that carries the brain, the seat of intellect and thought. But the crown rests *above* the head, beyond thought. What can be greater than intellect? Desire. In Hebrew, this is called *ratzon.* Desire is a mighty force, inviting us to explore possibilities that rationality would show to be wrong or difficult.

---

6 *Zohar III*, 11b.

7 7:86.

8 Literally "weighing ten *[shekels]* apiece."

9 The seven statutes of Rabbinic law are: lighting the Shabbos and Holiday candles, reading the *Megillah* on Purim, lighting Chanukah candles, washing one's hands before partaking of bread, the blessings before eating, the *eruv,* and the recitation of *Hallel* on holidays.

10 *Shabbos* 104a.

Say, for example, you'd like to become successful in a certain occupation. Even though you may have failed every class in school, you can persevere and succeed if you have the will and desire. Why? Because you *want* to. The power, the crown, of desire is so potent that it has the ability to transcend and actually transform your intellect.

In turn, there's another concept that even transcends desire, and that is pleasure (*tainug*). If a person derives pleasure from something he will automatically gravitate toward it. As a result he will mobilize his intellect and devise a strategy to attain it. That's why *kesser* is represented by the letter *kaf*—twenty—to teach us that there are two levels, or faculties, within the crown: desire and pleasure, with each faculty containing ten aspects. These aspects are also known as the ten holy *Sefiros* (spheres),[11] the ten building blocks of Creation. Three of the ten levels reside in the dimension of the intellect—Wisdom, Understanding, and Knowledge—and seven occupy the dimension of the emotions—Love, Fear, Mercy, Victory, Praise (Acknowledgment), Foundation (Bonding), and Sovereignty (Speech). The two faculties of the crown of *kaf*—pleasure and desire—twice encompass the three levels of intellect and seven levels of emotion for a total of twenty levels.

It states in the *Talmud*[12] that the crown of Torah is *halachah*—law. Why is it specifically law (i.e., those things that we should and shouldn't do) that is considered the crown of Torah? For the answer we can look to the reason G-d gave us the Torah. We did not receive the Torah to have some nice stories to entertain ourselves with, to read to our kids as a bedtime story, or to analyze in a literature class. On the contrary, the purpose of Torah is that we carry out His law, i.e., that we fulfill G-d's desire and in so doing give Him pleasure.

11 *Tanya*, chs. 3, 5; *Iggeres HaKodesh*, Epistle 15.
12 *Megillah* 28b. Also see *Tanya*, *Iggeres HaKodesh*, Epistle 29.

It therefore states in the *Talmud*: "Great is the study of Torah, for it brings to action."[13] Like the crown, Torah's ultimate purpose is to go beyond the head, beyond the intellect, and propel us to act in accordance with G-d's will, thus refining us as people and completing G-d's purpose in Creation.

Meaning

One of the meanings of the letter *kaf* is "spoon." The root of the word "spoon" is *kafaf*–to bend. As we discussed earlier, the *kaf* is a letter that is bent. It represents the aspect of submitting oneself to a greater power.

This notion of submission—and humility—can be seen clearly in the difference between the words *anochi* and *ani*. Both mean "I." When a person walks around all day and says, "I, I, I," he has a problem with egotism. How does one overcome this self-inflation? By adding a *kaf* to the אני (*ani*), the I, and transforming it into the אנכי (*anochi*). When the "I" submits to G-d, when it recognizes and bends to the higher power through the *kaf*, it is no longer the egotistical I. Rather, אנכי (*anochi*) is the "I" that serves as a channel to do G-d's will.[14]

There are actually two *kafs*. There's the bent *kaf* (כ), and the straight, or final, *kaf* (ך). What's the difference?

We explained previously that *Kesser*, the king's crown, is comprised of two levels: pleasure and desire. It has also been described as representing the internal and external aspects of the king. In this case, internal refers to the king's relation to himself, while external is his relationship to the world, his kingdom. Regarding the king's internal aspect—he doesn't necessarily want to be king, to be under the thumb of the ceaseless demands of his position. He wants to live within the boundaries of his own will, the internal world of study, erudi-

---

13 *Kiddushin* 40b.
14 *Sefer HaMaamarim 5703*, p. 197.

tion, spirituality, and family. This is the meaning of the passage[15] "From his shoulders up he was taller than the rest of his people," that is, secluded from the people.

The king's crown, however, also demands the straight *kaf*, which unfurls to reach down to his subjects; the external level of the king's existence. He's required to interact, to be responsible and benevolent to his kingdom.

The bent *kaf* therefore represents the introverted or inverted king—who remains isolated within his internalized world. The straight *kaf* (similar to the *vav*) represents the king who descends from his high level and reaches down to others in order to communicate with and rule his people.

Interestingly enough, we observe that when you affix the straight *kaf* as the suffix to a word, it adds the word "you" to the root. As it says:[16] "I will exalt *You* (ארוממך) my G-d the King." When you speak directly to a person, you say "you": *lecha*, לך, or *becha*, בך—spelled with a straight *kaf*. The final *kaf* thus *literally* unfolds to include the person to whom you are speaking. It represents the fact that the king has appeared to us and we are able to speak to him face to face.

The letter *kaf*. To bend oneself. To submit to the crown—the King, G-d, the ruler of the universe.

15 *I Samuel* 9:2.
16 *Psalms* 145:1.

לערנ(ען)

ליכט

Lamed

LAMED—TEACHERS AND STUDENTS

Design	*Kaf* and *vav*
Gematria	Thirty and 26
Meaning	**1.** Learn **2.** teach

I was having a hard time disciplining one of my children. Whatever I tried didn't work. I would tell him, "You will be punished, I won't give you a Chanukah present, I will not buy you any toys this year for your birthday...." To no avail.

One day, while I was standing with my family in a shopping center, my son began seriously misbehaving. I knew that my previous threats had proved to be futile and decided to try another strategy. To get his attention, I took out some lollipops and gave them to my other children, but not to him. He started to scream and demanded to know why he didn't get one. I knelt down and looked at him with compassion. "When a child gets a lollipop," I said softly, "it is a reward for his good behavior. I know you are a good boy so I know you will soon show me that you deserve the lollipop." This approach caught him off guard. He instantly calmed down, gave me a smile... and put out his hand for the lollipop. I then realized that one can teach discipline with love and kindness rather than with hate or anger. You just have to raise yourself to a higher consciousness. My son also learned a valuable lesson: that expressing a desirable quality is much more rewarding than misbehaving.

Design

The twelfth letter of the *alef-beis* is the *lamed*. The design of the *lamed* is two letters merged together[1]: the *vav* and the *kaf*.[2] The *Kabbalah*[3] says that the letter *lamed* is compared to a tower flying in the air.

---

1   *Sefer HaLikkutim, Osios,* letter *lamed,* written by the Tzemach Tzedek, the third Rebbe of *Chabad* (1789-1866).

2   *Reshimos* #53, p. 6.

3   See *Sefer HaLikkutim, loc. cit.,* pp. 845; 847.

Gematria

The *gematria* of *lamed* is thirty. It states in *Ethics of Our Fathers*: "When one reaches the age of thirty, he reaches the age of full strength."[4] We find in the Torah that when the Jewish people were in the desert, the Levites who carried the heavy vessels had to be between the ages of thirty to fifty, for these are the mightiest years of man.

What was the underlying purpose of the Jews' journeying forty years in the desert? On one hand, we know that it was the result of the sin of the Spies. The Spies' forty-day turn in the Land of Israel evoked G-d's decree to remain in the desert for forty years.[5] But why did they specifically have to *wander* throughout the desert? Why not stay in one place? Set up camp and stay there for forty years. What was the reason for having to undertake a total of forty-two different journeys in forty years?

The purpose of the Jewish people's travels in the desert was to transform it into a garden; to bring G-dliness to a desolate place. By carrying with them the Holy Ark—and within it the Torah—each and every one of the Jews' encampments became not only a spiritual but a literal garden. This became a lesson and guidepost for the Jewish people in all their future exiles. G-d was informing them: Throughout history, you will have to travel. You'll trek from country to country to country. But wherever you go, you must take the Ark of G-d with you—ushering G-dliness to that area, elevating it and making its inhabitants more refined and spiritual. This is the purpose of a Jew.[6]

This power to begin transforming the world in earnest begins when we turn thirty. Up until that point we are in training. The

---

4 5:23.
5 *Numbers* 14:34. See also chapter on the letter *yud*.
6 *Likkutei Torah*, beginning of *Naso* and p. 22b. *Likkutei Sichos*, vol. 13, pp. 16-17.

Midrash Shmuel[7] states that one has the ability to guide and influence others for good at the age of thirty. Until then, he is simply laying his foundation.

We find another interesting *gematria* in relation to *lamed*. Both the *alef* (in the form of the word *ulfana*) and the *lamed* (as in *lameid*) represent G-d as a teacher. What's the connection between the two letters? The design of the *alef* is comprised of two *yuds* and a *vav*: 10 and 10 and 6=26. The *lamed* is comprised of a *kaf* and a *vav*: 20 and 6=26. Twenty-six is the *gematria* of G-d's name, the Tetragrammaton *Yud-Hei-Vav-Hei*.

Yet there is a marked difference between the teaching styles of the *alef* and the *lamed*. The *alef* is more theoretical while the *lamed* is more practical. For example, the *alef* represents the Written Law of Torah (stories and general concepts) while the *lamed* focuses on the Oral Law (how to practically apply these concepts in one's day-to-day behavior).[8]

In another source, the Rebbe writes[9] that the *kaf* of the *lamed* represents the human being, which is comprised of a G-dly soul and animal soul, each of which is comprised of ten faculties (equaling twenty). The *vav* represents G-d dwelling between them. The numerical value of the *kaf* is twenty. When G-d dwells between them, He adds His Ten *Sefiros*, or G-dly energies, making thirty, which is *lamed*.

This is perhaps why the *Zohar* calls the *lamed* a tower flying in the air. The *vav* of the *lamed* represents G-dliness, spirituality, found high up "in the air." The *vav*, which is a chute, draws this G-dliness down from the spiritual realms into the physical world, until it is internalized into the *kaf*, the human being. This

---

7 *Ethics of Our Fathers* 5:22.

8 *Alef*, being the first letter, represents the first step toward acquiring knowledge, and is therefore more theoretical. The letter *lamed* appears toward the middle of the *alef-beis*, and is thus deeper into the process. At this point, you are ready to translate the theoretical knowledge into more practical applications.

9 *Reshimos* #53, p. 6.

merging of spiritual and physical imbues the *lamed* with the ability to teach very lofty concepts in a practical way.

Meaning

Lamed means to learn and to teach—found in the daily prayers with the phrase *lilmod u'lameid*.[10] But the word *lamed*, the commandment to teach, is not directed merely toward schoolteachers, it is a directive for *every* individual. Every person can influence his or her friend or student, and every parent has the obligation to teach his or her children the knowledge of G-d, good deeds and ethics. The Torah tells us[11] that "You shall teach your children and talk to them about these things" (i.e., the Torah's commandments and responsibilities). The *Rambam* informs us that this passage is the premise for the *mitzvah* of *talmud Torah*, Torah study; that through the commandment to teach our children, we know of our own obligation to study the Torah. For how can we teach our children the Torah if we haven't learned it ourselves?

We can all ask a simple question: Why do we have to learn about this most essential commandment indirectly? If G-d wanted to tell us that we are obligated to learn Torah, why didn't He just say, "Learn Torah!" Why do we have to learn about this *mitzvah* by way of the commandment "Teach your children"?

The Rebbe[12] explains that when it comes to studying Torah, a person is *always* a child, and thus the commandment to "teach your children" can also apply to us. One should never say, "Oh, I'm fifty now. I've read through the Torah more than twenty times. You can't teach me anything new." On the contrary, Torah is infinite. No matter how many times we've set foot in it,

10 Blessing before the *Shema*.
11 *Deuteronomy* 6:7.
12 *Likkutei Sichos*, vol. 19, p. 38ff.

we can always discover a new insight or uncover deeper meaning. We must approach it like children, and be ready to receive and listen. As it states in *Ethics of Our Fathers:*[13] "Who is wise? One who learns from everyone." "Everyone" can mean even someone who's younger than you.

Even your children.

13 4:1.

מ ם

מבול
מים

Mem

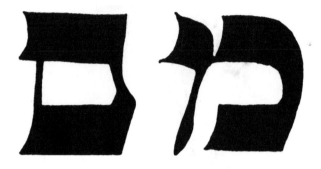

MEM—METAMORPHOSIS

Design	1. Open *mem*—revealed Torah; closed *mem*—concealed Torah 2. closed *mem*—period of gestation; open *mem*—childbirth
Gematria	Forty
Meaning	1. Water 2. *Mashiach*

When the *mikveh* in Brownsville, N.Y. wanted to close its doors because of financial difficulties, my mother's paternal great-grandfather, Hersh-Meilech Hecht, volunteered to take over all the financial responsibilities and practical duties. In 1929, the sixth Lubavitcher Rebbe, Rabbi Yosef Yitzchak Schneersohn, came to visit the Jews in America. The chassidim asked him to deliver a *maamar*, a Chassidic discourse. He responded that he must first immerse in a *mikveh*, a ritual bath. Normally, my grandfather charged ten cents for usage of the facilities, but not when a Rebbe used it. When he heard the Lubavitcher Rebbe was coming, he prepared the room in honor of the Rebbe as one would for a king.

On the way out of the *mikveh*, the Rebbe handed him a five-dollar bill (a lot of money in those days). Hersh-Meilech refused to take the money and asked for a blessing instead. The Rebbe blessed him and said, "Your grandchildren will become my chassidim and will learn in (my *yeshivah*) *Tomchei Temimim*." And so it came to pass.

Design

The letter *mem* is the thirteenth letter of the *alef-beis*.

There are two forms of the *mem*: the open *mem* and the closed *mem*. As the *Talmud* explains,[1] the open *mem* represents the revealed Torah and the closed *mem* represents the Torah's secrets.

The *AriZal* states:[2] "It is a *mitzvah* to reveal the secrets of Torah." Being that we now find ourselves in the Messianic era, it is not just permitted, it is an *obligation* to experience a foretaste of the teachings of *Mashiach*, which are the secrets of the Torah. This level of Torah is represented by the closed *mem*.

---

1 *Shabbos* 104a.
2 Introduction to *Eitz Chayim*; *Shaar HaGilgulim*, end of *Shaar HaHakdomos* 16; *Hilchos Talmud Torah*, 1:4; *Tanya, Iggeres HaKodesh*, Epistle 26; *et al.*

The *Rambam* begins his first book, the *Mishneh Torah*, with a section of laws entitled "The Foundations of Torah." In this section, he discusses G-d, the angels, and the heavens, and explains: "This that I told you up until now is called 'the secrets of Creation and the secrets of the Chariot.'"[3] These mystical insights are complex Kabbalistic concepts. Yet the *Rambam* decided to teach them as a foundation—a prerequisite for everyone who studies the Torah.[4] The apprehension of G-d's awesomeness, of His stirring and unfathomable ways, must precede even the essential laws of the revealed Torah, such as the *Shema*, Shabbos and *tefillin*.

Additionally, the *mem* represents the womb[5]—רחם (*rechem*)—which ends with a closed *mem*. The closed *mem* represents the nine months when the womb is closed. The open *mem* represents the period of childbirth, when the womb is open.

Gematria

The *gematria* of *mem* is forty. Forty is the number of days it rained upon the earth during the Flood. Forty is also the number of days Moses spent on Mount Sinai. Moses actually ascended the mountain three separate times. The first forty-day sojourn took place when he received the Torah. Then Moses descended with the Tablets, but shattered them when he saw the Golden Calf that the people had made in his absence. The following morning Moses returned to the mountain for another forty days to pray on behalf of the Jewish people. When Moses

3 In Hebrew, *Maaseh HaMerkavah*. The mystical interpretations of G-d's heavenly chariot as expressed in the vision of the prophet Ezekiel.

4 In his Introduction to the *Mishneh Torah*, the *Rambam* writes: "After one learns the Five Books of Moses... look immediately into my book. For I am writing it for the young and for the old." Since the *Mishneh Torah* discusses the secrets of Torah, and a ten-year-old child begins to learn it right after he learns *Chumash*, he is learning mysticism from the very beginning of his studies.

5 *Sefer HaArachim Chabad, Osios*, letter *mem*, p. 176, Kehot Publication Society, Brooklyn, NY.

returned to the encampment, G-d called out[6] for him to return to the mountain, this time, with his own tablets. So Moses dug under his tent and found two sapphire stones.[7] He brought them up with him to Mount Sinai for the third and final forty days, and G-d engraved the Ten Commandments on them.[8] It was the tenth of the month of Tishrei when Moses came down from the mountain with G-d's law after these final forty days. G-d declared, "I have forgiven [the Jewish people] as you have asked." The culmination of these three forty-day periods, the tenth of Tishrei, Yom Kippur, is thus the day we as the Jewish people fast and pray to atone for our sins.

There are other significant references to forty in the Torah: Moses' spies scouted the land for forty days. The Jews were in the desert for forty years. And a *mikveh*, a ritual bath, is made up of forty *se'ah* (about 200 gallons).

What is the concept of forty? Forty represents a metamorphosis,[9] a transformation. After forty days, the embryo of a child begins to assume a recognizable form.[10]

Additionally, a *mikveh* (with its forty *se'ah*) has the ability to change an individual from a state of impurity to purity. And if one wants to undertake a conversion,[11] one must immerse in a *mikveh*, whereupon his or her Jewish soul is revealed.

G-d brought a flood upon this world for forty days and forty nights. The waters of the flood were not for revenge, as is commonly assumed, but for atonement, to purify and transform the world, in much the same way a *mikveh* purifies a person.[12]

Each of Moses' forty-day sojourns in heaven signified a transformation. The first forty days was to receive the Torah,

6 *Deuteronomy* 10:1.
7 *Exodus* 34:1. See *Rashi* on verse.
8 There is another opinion that states that Moshe carved the Second Tablets himself.
9 *Biurim L'Iggeres HaTeshuvah*, ch.2.
10 Medically, it takes approximately forty days to detect a heartbeat in a human embryo.
11 *Rambam, Laws of Prohibited Relations*, 13:1.
12 *Torah Or, Noach*, p. 8d; *Likkutei Sichos*, vol. 1, p. 4.

and when an individual learns Torah, he or she develops the ability to change for the better. The second trip was for prayer, *tefillah*. When a person prays, he or she can change an evil decree; in this case, G-d's intention to annihilate the Jewish people. Indeed, because of Moses' supplications, G-d was willing to bestow His mercy and once again offer them His Torah. The final ascent represented *teshuvah* (repentance)—also a transformation—because once a person has repented, he is no longer the same person he was when he sinned. When Moses finally returned to the Jewish people with G-d's law, they were at a level of atonement—and thus finally prepared to become G-d's nation.

Furthermore, the words Torah, *tefillah* and *teshuvah* begin with a *tav*, which has the numerical value of 400, or 40x10 (i.e., serving G-d with all of one's 10 faculties for 40 days).

The forty years that the Jews spent in the desert also constituted a transformation. The nation that had rebelled against G-d had metamorphosed into a nation that was ready to adhere to His word.

Meaning

The word *mem* stands for *mayim*, which means water. Water constitutes a vital element in our lives: a human being is largely composed of water and the majority of the earth is covered with it.

Torah, the most vital element in our spiritual lives, is referred to as water, as it states: "*Ein* mayim *ela Torah*[13]—There is no water but Torah." As the Prophet tells us,[14] "He who is thirsty shall go and drink water," meaning that a Jew's thirst for spirituality will never be sated by looking to other cultures or

---

13 *Bava Kamma* 82a.
14 *Isaiah* 55:1.

religions. The only thing that will quench one's thirst is water, which is Torah.

Just as a fish cannot survive without water, a Jew cannot survive without Torah. The story is told of a fish and a fox.[15] The fish was busy evading a fisherman's net when he spied a fox standing on the shore of the lake. The fox called out to the fish and said, "Little fish, where are you going?" The fish answered, "The fishermen are all trying catch me, so I'm trying to swim away!" Feigning concern, the conniving fox offered, "Little fish, come up out of the water. I will protect you." Replied the fish, "Silly fox. In the water I still have a chance. But once I leave the water, I will surely die."

A Jew without Torah is like a fish without water. Of course we know that the water isn't without its difficulties. There is anti-Semitism. We run from country to country, trying to survive a Spanish Inquisition and a Holocaust. Yet even amidst the onslaught, we have persevered as a people. The moment we leave our culture, the moment we leave the water—our connection to G-d and Torah—we are spiritually dead.

Torah is also compared to water because water travels unaltered from the top of a mountain to its lower tiers and valleys. So did G-d bring down the same deep, intellectual Torah He had in heaven to the physical world. The *Zohar* says that G-d looked into the Torah to create the world. The Torah serves as a blueprint for Creation. The wealth and strength of its water carves, and continues to carve out the foundation of the entire world.

The *Mishnah*, the Oral Law of Torah, begins and ends with the letter *mem*. Its first word is *M'eimasai*[16] and its concluding word is *bashalom*,[17] "peace." Furthermore, the *Rambam*[18] also

15 *Berachos* 61b.
16 *Ibid.* 1:1.
17 The last *mishnah* in *Uksin.*
18 *Yein Malchus,* Epistle 1.

begins and ends his great work, the *Mishneh Torah*, with a *mem*—beginning the first chapter with the word *Meshoch*, and concluding the final volume with the word *mechasim*.

The *mem* also represents the womb. In essence, water is the womb of Creation. The Torah begins,[19] "In the beginning G-d created the heavens and the earth." The next verse states that before G-d created the heavens and the earth "...the spirit of G-d hovered over the waters."[20] What waters? Since the earth's waters had not yet been created, the waters mentioned here are the womb from which Creation emerged, the place of gestation before the world came into existence.

Mikveh embodies this concept as well. When one immerses in a *mikveh*, it is similar to entering the womb of Creation, a state of the world yet unborn. At the moment when the person emerges, he or she is reborn. On a more practical level, the individual submerged in a *mikveh* is in a medium where he or she can't survive and will ultimately die. When the individual emerges from the water, he or she is renewed.[21] The word *mikveh* also begins with the letter *mem*.[22]

It states in *Isaiah*:[23] "*L'marbei hamisra u'leshalom*," which means, "His rule (i.e., the kingship of *Mashiach*) will increase and be blessed with peace without end." Throughout the entire Torah, the final form of the *mem* appears in the middle of a word only once—here, in the word לסרבה, *l'marbei*. What is the

---

19 *Genesis* 1:1.

20 *Ibid.* 1:2.

21 See Aryeh Kaplan, *Waters of Eden: The Mystery of Mikvah*, NCSY/Union of Orthodox Jewish Congregations of America, NY, 1982, pp. 72-73.

22 *HaYom Yom*, entry for 10 Nissan, "On the subject of the campaign to popularize the observance of family purity in your community, ponder this deeply: Let us imagine that G-d were to give you the opportunity to save a Jewish community from extinction (G-d forbid), you would certainly be willing to risk your life for this and you would thank and praise Him for His great kindness in offering you an opportunity of such enormous merit. The same then holds true to an even greater degree with regard to the campaign for *taharat hamishpacha*; it is an endeavor which literally saves lives."

23 9:6.

significance of this? That *Mashiach* will bring closure to the exile. We discussed earlier that the three lines of the letter *beis*—two horizontal and one vertical—represent three directions (or corners) of the earth. The north side, that which is open to evil, remains unresolved. With the arrival of *Mashiach*, the fourth side of the *beis* of *Bereishis*—Creation—is completed and the letter *beis* is transformed into a *mem*.[24] And the emergence of this form of the *mem* in turn facilitates the consummation of its very own design, whereby the closed *mem*—the hidden or secret aspects of Torah—takes the place of the open *mem*, the revealed aspects of the Torah. For along with the everlasting peace of *Mashiach* will come the explanation of the reasons for the exile, and the pain and suffering of the Jewish people that accompanied it.

וי אַ פֿישׁ אִין װאַסער

Nun

NUN—MASHIACH

Design	1. Bent *nun*—serves G-d out of fear (awe); Straight *nun*—serves G-d out of love 2. Bent *nun*—he who has fallen; Straight *nun*—he who has risen 3. He who is bent over in this world will stand straight in the World to Come
Gematria	Fifty
Meaning	1. Deceit 2. kingship 3. fish 4. miscarriage 5. miracle

A story is told in the *Talmud*:[1] Rabbi Yehoshua ben Levi meets Elijah the Prophet and asks, "When will *Mashiach* come?"

Elijah responds, "Why are you asking me? You can ask *Mashiach* himself."

"Really?! Where can I find *Mashiach*?"

Elijah tells him, "Go to the gates of Rome and there you'll find him."

Rabbi Yehoshua ben Levi thinks for a moment. "Fine, but there are many people at the gates of Rome. How will I know which one is *Mashiach*?"

"He will be sitting amongst the poor people who are enduring pain and suffering."

So Rabbi Yehoshua ben Levi presses, "There are many people suffering and in pain. How will I know who *Mashiach* is?"

Elijah concludes, "All the other sufferers will be unwrapping their bandages in one continuous motion. *Mashiach*, however, will remove and reapply one bandage at a time, strip by strip."

What does he mean, "strip by strip"? The people who are suffering from disease and injury tie and untie their bandages at the same time. But *Mashiach* wraps one finger, one joint, one wound at a time. This is because when *Mashiach* is finally called, he won't even wait for the blink of an eye. He won't have to take the time to finish reapplying a lengthy bandage. He'll be able to save his people *immediately.*

So Rabbi Yehoshua proceeds to the gates of Rome and finds *Mashiach* there. He says, "*Nu!* When are you going to come?"

Mashiach answers, "Today."

1 *Sanhedrin* 98a.

"*Today*?! That's great!" And he runs back home, packs his bags, and tells the entire town, "*Mashiach* is coming today!" And so they wait. The people are waiting and waiting but the sun finally sets and *Mashiach* never shows up. A few days pass. Again Yehoshua ben Levi meets up with Elijah. Elijah says, "*Nu*, you met *Mashiach*? What do you think of him?"

Reb Yehoshua responds, "He lied to me!"

"What are you talking about?" says Elijah.

"Well, I asked him, 'When are you coming?' He said he's coming *today,* but he never showed up."

Elijah interjects, "I'm sorry. I don't think you heard him correctly. He [was quoting the verse]: "'Today, *if* you will hearken to My voice,'"[2] [and then continued with:] 'If you will return to G-d and follow the laws of the Torah, I will come. Until then I'm waiting.'"

Design

The fourteenth letter of the *alef-beis* is the *nun.*

There are two types of *nun*s. The "bent" *nun* (*nun kefufah*) either begins or is in the middle of a word. The straight, or final *nun* (*nun peshutah*), is employed only at a word's end. The *Talmud*[3] tells us that the *nun kefufah* represents one who is bent over and the *nun peshutah* is one who is straight.

The *Maharal* explains[4] that the two *nun*s represent the two fundamental approaches to serving G-d: fear and love. The first person serves G-d out of awe, fear. Therefore, he is hunched over. The second person serves G-d out of love and thus stands straight. This person is also characterized by generosity, because love represents openness.

---

2 *Psalms* 95:7.

3 *Shabbos* 104a.

4 *The Wisdom in the Hebrew Alphabet, op. cit.,* p. 152.

Another interpretation is found in the work of the *Shelah*,[5] where it states that the bent *nun* alludes to one who has fallen and the straight *nun* to one who has straightened back up.

Rashi comments that if a person is "bent over" throughout his life, that means he is humble. He is subservient to law and order, to Torah and to G-d. In the World to Come he will stand tall and straight, for G-d will bless him with tremendous reward.

It is interesting to note[6] that in a *halachic* debate, the final verdict in Jewish law isn't necessarily bestowed upon the one who is the more intelligent. Rather it is decided based on the opinion of the person who is the more humble. What does the Torah tell us about Moses? Not that he was a brilliant scholar, but that he was the epitome of humility.

The same is true of Joshua, Moses' successor. As some sources compare Moses to a fish, a *nun*,[7] because he was taken out of the water by Pharaoh's daughter, so is Joshua called "*ben Nun*," the son (disciple) of this great fish (Moses). Torah does not inform us about his intellect, but rather that he was Moses' disciple—that he was always at Moses' side and in Moses' tent. Why did he merit inheriting the leadership of the Jewish people from Moses? Because he embraced the quality of humility with his entire being.

Even before King David became king he was known as "the final verdict."[8] King Saul, his predecessor, was brilliant, but the *halachah* was determined according to David. We know that David was very humble; he is called "the servant of the L-rd"

---

5 Rabbi Isaiah Horowitz (1560-1630), renowned *halachist* and Kabbalist, in *Mesechta Taanis,* p. 206a,b. Also see *Sefer HaSichos 5751,* vol. 1, pp. 387-388.

6 *Pelach HaRimon* 1:19a, by Reb Hillel of Paritch.

7 *The Alef-Beit, op. cit.,* p. 217. Also see *Bereishis Rabbah* 97:4-5.
   Note that Moshe was born in the month of Adar, which corresponds to *mazal dagim* or Pisces. In addition, *nun* means "fish" in Aramaic.

8 As it states in the *Talmud:* "G-d is with him." Why? Because "the law goes according to him." (*Sanhedrin* 93b)

and "My servant David."[9] Additionally, Hillel, the famous
Tannaic rabbi and scholar, faced off time and time again
against his colleague Shammai in determining Jewish law.
Shammai was actually intellectually sharper than Hillel, but the
halachah was decided according to Hillel because of his humility and kindness.

It states in the *HaYom Yom*:[10] "The unique quality of
Mashiach is that he will be humble. Though he will be the
ultimate in greatness—for he will teach Torah to the Patriarchs
and to Moses—so, too, he will be the ultimate in humility and
self-nullification, for he will also teach simple folk."

Whether one serves G-d out of love or fear, or whether one is
bent or straight, the spark of *Mashiach* found within all of us
will empower us with the humility to embrace the diversity of
creation.

Gematria

The *gematria* of *nun* is fifty. There are fifty "gates" or levels of
Binah, understanding. That's why the Jews counted forty-nine
days—seven complete weeks from Passover to Shavuos—to
ready themselves to receive the Torah. The famous question is,
why does the Torah tell us to count fifty days after Passover,
when immediately afterwards it says to count seven complete
weeks, which are only *forty-nine* days? The answer is that an
individual can only attain forty-nine levels of intellect on his
own. The fiftieth level, that of transcendence, can only be
provided by G-d. Therefore G-d says: You do yours and I will
do Mine. If you achieve the forty-ninth level, I will bless you
with the fiftieth; the highest tier of *Binah*, understanding.[11]

---

9 *Ezekiel* 34:24.
10 Entry for Menachem Av 1, *Rosh Chodesh*.
11 *Rosh Hashanah* 21b; also see *Pardes Rimonim, Shaar HaShaarim, Shaar 13*, ch. 1.

On the Jewish calendar, every fiftieth year is called the year of *Yovel*, or Jubilee. In the Jubilee year, all lands in the Land of Israel are "given their freedom," and returned to their original owners.

How is the concept of freedom and the Torah connected? In *Ethics of Our Fathers* it states: "One who learns Torah is truly free,"[12] but for the skeptic to challenge this statement would be all too easy. *"Free?!* What do you mean free? The Torah is full of restrictions! It tells me not to do this and not to do that. Some freedom!"

Yet indeed, when one learns Torah, he is free of the false, materialistic constraints of society. Free from his self-centered, animalistic inclinations. He has the power to confront and transcend these obstacles. Furthermore, Torah gives an individual the ability to maximize his potential, to be the best he can be.

As an example, when you are eating good, nutritious food, your performance is optimally enhanced. Sure, you can survive on brownies and Coca-Cola. But the fact of the matter is, when you eat healthful foods, you're able to produce better.

The same holds true regarding living according to the laws of Torah. Perhaps you believe you don't need the Torah in your life, that you can survive very well without it. After all, you have all the material amenities to live relatively stress-free, and your social life is in full swing. But when you *do* decide to live a Torah lifestyle, you soon realize that you're able to operate at a much higher plane of existence than the average individual. You feel that you are in control of your life and are not enslaved to the dictates of the false values of society.

12 6:2.

Meaning

The *Zohar*[13] tells us that the *nun* stands for *ona'ah*—deceit. To the human eye, this world seems to be controlled by the laws of nature, for one cannot see G-d. This false reality therefore is a total deception.

The mission for all of us is to reveal and draw G-d's infinite light down into this world,[14] so that we can see the true reality of the world—that everything is G-dliness and G-dliness is everything. This is done by cleaving to G-d and observing His commandments. This concept is expressed in the straight, long (final) *nun*,[15] which has a design similar to the *vav*, a chute. In contrast to the *vav*, however, its leg extends beneath the base-line. This implies the downward flow of Divine energy reaching into even the deepest abyss. This will ultimately happen with *Mashiach's* arrival.

Nun also means "kingship." There is a verse in *Tehillim* regarding *Mashiach* that states:[16] "May his name (Yinon) endure forever, as long as the sun." According to *Rashi*, Yinon refers to kingship. If we break the word "Yinon" into two—*yud* and *nun*—*nun* means kingship, and putting a *yud* before a word denotes continuity.[17] Therefore, the name Yinon implies that the kingship of *Mashiach* will endure forever.

In Aramaic, *nun* means a fish. Another meaning of *nun* is a *bar nafli*, one who has fallen, or a miscarriage. In the Torah portion entitled Balak,[18] the prophet Bilaam prophesizes the coming of two kings. The first one is King David. The second is

13 III, 180b.
14 G-d's infinite light, also known as the encompassing or transcendent light (*sovev kol almin*), cannot be perceived through the human senses. This light will be revealed, however, in the final stages of the Messianic Age, the Resurrection of the Dead.
15 *Likkutei Torah, Bamidbar*, p. 21a, and *Devarim*, p. 20b.
16 *Psalms* 72:17.
17 As explained in the chapter on *yud*.
18 *Deuteronomy* 30:3-5. *Rambam's Code of Jewish Law: Laws of Kings* 11:1.

King *Mashiach*, who will rise from David's descendants in the final days.

The *Midrash* states that David was originally supposed to have died through a miscarriage. He was able to survive only because Adam (the first man) bequeathed David seventy of his own years.[19] *Mashiach*, a descendant of David, is called a *bar nafli*,[20] literally translated as the "son of one who has fallen," or a miscarriage. A miscarriage causes great pain and suffering to the mother and to those close to her. The role of pain and suffering is an important element of *Mashiach's* presence on earth. Because he feels the suffering of the Jewish people, he will pray fervently on their behalf to bring redemption and healing.

King David is known as David ben Yishai—the son of Yishai. It is interesting to note that the *gematria* of בן ישי, "ben Yishai," is 372, the same value as the words בר נפלי, *bar nafli*.

The *Talmud*[21] tells us there was a debate over the name of *Mashiach*. One group said the name of *Mashiach* is Menachem. The other group said it's Shiloh. The third group said *Mashiach's* name is Yinon. The fourth group said Chanina. In essence, they were all correct. *Mashiach* (spelled *mem, shin, yud, ches*) is an acronym of all four names. The *mem* of *Mashiach* represents Menachem, which means consolation, for *Mashiach* will come and console the Jewish people and soothe their pain and anguish from the exile and the destruction of the First and Second Holy Temples. Then he will be Shiloh (*shin*), which means he will become king and reign over the people, restoring law and order. Shiloh, which also means "gifts to him," refers to one's obligation to bring presents to the king. Then he will be Yinon (*yud*), which means fish that multiply

19 Adam lived 930 years (*Genesis* 5:5). He was originally supposed to have lived for 1,000 years (*Zohar* I, p. 168a).

20 *Sanhedrin* 96b.

21 *Ibid.* 98b.

rapidly and endure. Under *Mashiach's* reign, the world will be fruitful and multiply. The last name is Chanina (*ches*). Chanina means *chein*, grace. *Mashiach* will ultimately bring grace, peace, and harmony to the world.

Furthermore, the *Talmud* tells us that a person who dreams "and sees Chanina"[22] is destined to witness "many, many" miracles, because there are two *nun*s in the word Chanina. The word *nun* also means *nes*, miracle. Two *nun*s denote *nisei nissim*: many, many miracles. In the era of *Mashiach*, everyone will witness great wonders and miracles.

In conclusion, *nun*, which represents humility, is the vessel for all of G-d's blessings. Intellectually, when one is humble, one acquires the fiftieth (and crowning) level of understanding; on a material level, one attains abundant material wealth through his ability to "multiply like a fish." Through our efforts to achieve humility, we will be blessed both materially and spiritually with the coming of *Mashiach*.

---

22 *Berachos* 56b.

Samech

SAMECH—TO SUPPORT AND HEAL

Design	1. Closed circle 2. wedding ring
Gematria	Sixty
Meaning	1. Support 2. medicine

Yaakov had been terribly ill for weeks. He finally decided to ask R. Mordechai of Neshchiz for advice. "Rebbe," he sobbed, "please help me. I am extremely sick. I have gone to every doctor in town, but none of them has a cure for me."

"It seems that you haven't gone to the right doctor," replied R. Mordechai. "Go immediately to Anipoli and talk to the specialist there. Then you will be cured."

Yaakov thanked the Rebbe for his advice, hired a wagon, and set out for Anipoli. When he arrived there, he rushed over to the first person he saw and asked, "Please, tell me where the great specialist lives. I am very ill and must see him right away."

The person was puzzled. "You came to Anipoli for a specialist?! This is such a small village, we don't even have a *doctor* here."

"You must be mistaken," Yaakov insisted. "R. Mordechai of Neshchiz explicitly told me to go to Anipoli and see the specialist here. You must tell me—where does he live?"

"But there is no doctor here," the man repeated.

Yaakov went to everyone in town, asking each the same question: "Where is the specialist? I must see the specialist right away." And everyone gave him the same answer: "There is no specialist in Anipoli. There is not even a doctor."

Disappointed and frustrated, Yaakov returned to R. Mordechai of Neshchiz. "Rebbe," he said, "I don't understand. You sent me to Anipoli, but the people told me that not only is there no specialist there, there is not even a doctor."

"Hmm. They don't even have a doctor?" questioned the Rebbe. "So did you ask the people what they do when someone is sick?"

"I did," Yaakov replied. "They told me that when someone is sick, they pray to G-d and rely on Him to cure them."

"Now do you understand?" R. Mordechai explained. "The people in Anipoli go to the greatest specialist in the world. They pray to G-d. He is the one Who cures us all."[1]

Design

The design of the *samech* is a closed circle. A circle represents infinity, because it has no beginning or end. In *Kabbalah* the *samech* represents the infinite power of the *Ein Sof*, G-d's infinite light. The *samech* also symbolizes an ambitious, enterprising individual.

The circular aspect of the *samech* represents support, like the rings that encircle and hold together all the elements of the *lulav*.[2]

The *samech* also resembles a wedding band. In a relationship, a husband and wife have a strong desire to be wholly bonded as well as an intermittent need to separate. Since a circle has no points of distinction, the many different aspects of marriage do not need to conflict with one another: they can be ultimately bound together within the same uninterrupted structure of the circle.

Finally, the ring symbolizes a couple's commitment to each other. A woman symbolizes her uncompromising support of her husband by circling him seven times under the *chuppah*. Similarly, the man's commitment is symbolized by the giving of a ring. When you pick up someone who has fallen, you support and encircle him or her. With the wedding ring we are saying in effect, "This ring has no beginning or end, no highs or lows. The characteristic of encircling is constant. So, too, will my

---

1 From *A Treasury of Chassidic Tales, op. cit.* (Author's Note: Of course one must do everything he or she can to find the best doctors suitable for one's ailment. However, we must realize that it is G-d working *through* that doctor that effects a person's healing.)

2 The *mitzvah* of "*lulav* and *esrog*" performed during the holiday of Sukkos consists of combining a date palm branch, myrtle twigs and willows into one entity called the *lulav*, and joining it with a citron (*esrog*) while making a series of prescribed movements.

commitment to you be constant, encompassing your whole being, regardless of the highs and lows of the relationship."

We find the same concept regarding the Jewish people who were married to G-d at Mount Sinai. The *Talmud*[3] states that the Giving of the Torah at Sinai "was the betrothal ceremony" when G-d gave us the ring, our wedding band. At that time we committed ourselves to follow G-d's laws, "and G-d then obligated Himself to provide the Jewish people with sustenance and livelihood."[4]

Gematria

The numerical value of the *samech*, the fifteenth letter of the *alef-beis*, is sixty. In the Priestly Blessing[5] recited every morning there are fifteen words and sixty letters. When the *kohen* blesses the people,[6] he must put his two hands together. According to the *Mishnah* there are thirty bones in each hand, sixty when the hands are joined.

What is unique about the Priestly Blessing? The results of such blessings are swift and without interruption, similar to the strength of a current of mighty water that no dam can stop. The Priestly Blessings embody the concept of the *samech*: infinite light and power.

A *halachah* regarding *kashrus* is an example of *samech's* strength. Suppose someone is cooking a big *cholent*[7] full of meat and needs to prepare a bottle of milk for his or her baby. A drop of milk accidentally falls into the pot. Is the *cholent* now

---

3 *Taanis* 26b.

4 See *HaYom Yom*, entry for Tishrei 28 [regarding the verse, *Vayikra* 26:3-4:] "If you go in My statutes... I will give your rains in their season...."

On a practical note, this means that if the Jewish people study Torah and observe *mitzvos*, G-d will provide them with sustenance and livelihood (symbolized by the all-encompassing blessing of rain).

5 *Numbers* 6:23. Also see *Siddur Tehillat Hashem*, p. 10, *et al.*

6 For a Chassidic insight into this *mitzvah*, see *Derech Mitzvosecha* (of the *Tzemach Tzedek*), pp. 223-224. Kehot Publication Society, Brooklyn, NY, 1991.

7 A hot stew of meat, potatoes and beans traditionally eaten on Shabbos day.

unkosher? The law states that if there is sixty times the amount of *cholent* to the one drop of milk, then the error is completely nullified. The ratio of this nullification is one to sixty, and is the origin of the term *batel beshishim* ("nullified by sixty").

It is interesting to note that the word *ayin*, which means "nothing," reiterates this concept when the value of its letters are added: *alef* = 1, *yud* = 10, and *nun* = 50, equaling 61. One to sixty is like nothing.

Other significant connections to sixty: King Solomon had sixty of his finest men surrounding his bed every night for protection. The *Mishnah* has sixty tractates. Sleep is one-sixtieth of death; a dream is one-sixtieth of prophecy; fire is one-sixtieth of hell; and honey constitutes one-sixtieth of the manna.

Being the fifteenth letter of the *alef-beis*, the *samech* shares an interesting connection to marriage through the number fifteen. The *Talmud*[8] states: "There were never greater days of joy for the Jewish people than the fifteenth of Av." On the fifteenth of the month of Av the single girls of Israel would go out into the field and dance in a circle (a *samech*) and sing, "Boys, pick up your eyes and look and find yourself a wife." Since a man and woman joined in marriage represents the greatest oneness and therefore the greatest joy in the world, this joy can be attributed to the circle of the *samech*.

The Rebbe says that the fifteenth of Av is the day that gives us a taste of the revelation that will accompany *Mashiach* and the rebuilding of the third Holy Temple.[9] We are told that the fifteenth of any month is the zenith of the Jewish calendar since the Jewish people are compared to the moon, and on the fifteenth the moon is full. The fifteenth of Av is the pinnacle of the month of Av. Since the descent in Av is the lowest on the

8 *Taanis* 26b.
9 *Sefer HaMaamarim Meluket*, vol. IV, p. 348.

calendar (the destruction of both Temples on the Ninth of Av), then the resulting ascent, the fifteenth of Av, is the highest day on the calendar.[10]

Av is actually spelled אב, *alef-beis*. This hints that the greatest letter in the *alef-beis* is the *samech*. The greatest day of the year, the 15th of Av, can also be read the 15th (letter) of the *alef-beis*.[11]

If there is one day that could surpass the elation of husband and wife finding each other, it would be the coming of *Mashiach* and the rebuilding of the Temple—the supreme union and *reunion* of the Jewish people and G-d. As it states in the *Talmud*:[12] "[At that time] G-d will make a circle for all the righteous [like a *samech*] and He will sit among them. Every one of them will point with his finger and say, 'This is our G-d...we have awaited Him and He is here to save us. ...Let us exalt and be glad in His salvation.'"[13]

Meaning

The word *samech* means "to support," as it states in the *Shemoneh Esreh*:[14] "*Someich noflim*—You support those who fall." It is not by chance that the *samech* follows the *nun* in the *alef-beis*. As mentioned earlier, the *nun* is one who has fallen, and as such, needs the *samech* to be supported or lifted up. On the other side of the *nun* is the *mem*, which also bolsters it. But the *samech* is greater than the *mem*. Every day we say in the morning blessings[15] that G-d is *Someich noflim*—He supports those who fall. We also say that He is *Zokeif kefufim* (with the *mem* appearing at the end of the phrase)—He straightens those

---

10 *HaYom Yom*, entry for 15 Av.
11 *The Alef-Beit, op cit.*, p. 228.
12 *Taanis* 31a.
13 *Isaiah* 25:9.
14 The *Amidah* prayer, the focal point of the prayer service.
15 *Psalms* 145.

who are bent. While the *mem* signifies the straightening of one who is bent, the *samech* can bear the weight of those who have entirely fallen.

The first two letters of the word *samech* are סמ—*samech-mem*. Together they spell the word *sam*, which means a potion or medicine. This is not only relevant with regard to one's physical health but also one's spiritual health. The word *samech* סמך is an acronym for: *salach* סלח, to forgive; *mechal* מחל, to pardon; and *kaper* כפר, to atone. When one takes strides to forgive, pardon and atone, one achieves a great spiritual healing.

It is also said that the *samech* and the *mem* represent two distinct eras.[16] The closed *mem* represents *Gan Eden*, Paradise (which is concealed from the human eye), the world of souls which currently exists in another dimension. The *samech* (which is greater than the *mem*) represents the era of *Techiyas HaMeisim*, the Resurrection of the Dead.[17] This is the ultimate manifestation of *Mashiach's* coming, when all the souls of the departed will return to bodily form and reside on earth for all time.

In the World to Come, the ring of the *samech* becomes even greater than its original function of supporting the fallen. For then it will radiate the infinite, transcendent healing which will last for eternity.

---

16 *Sefer HaArachim Chabad, Osios,* letter *samech,* p. 238.
17 While the *mem* represents *Mashiach,* the *samech* represents *sovev kol almin,* G-d's infinite light that will be revealed at the time of the Resurrection of the Dead.

כבן שבעים שנה

Ayin

AYIN—LEADERSHIP

Design	1. A *vav* in a *nun*
	2. two eyes connected to the optic nerve
Gematria	Seventy
Meaning	1. Eyes 2. salvation

Rabbi Elazar ben Azaryah was asked to become the *Nasi* (head) of a prestigious Torah Academy. After discussing the opportunity with his wife, she said, "But you have no white hair (i.e., you're only eighteen years old)! It's disrespectful for such a young man to lead the entire Academy." Now, what is a sign of someone old enough to be worthy of respect? White hair. That day, a miracle occurred and eighteen rows of hair in Rabbi Elazar ben Azaryah's beard turned white.[1]

This is why, after accepting the position, R. Elazar ben Azaryah began his opening address with the words, "I am *like* seventy years old," and not "I *am* seventy years old."

Design

The *ayin* is the sixteenth letter of the *alef-beis*. According to the *AriZal*, the *ayin* is a *vav* contained in a *nun*. The *nun* represents humility. The *vav* signifies Torah, which descends from Heaven to earth in its inherent design of a hook or a chute. *Vav* also has the *gematria* of six. This represents the Six Orders of the *Mishnah*, the Oral Law. Only an individual who is unassuming, who has the humility of the *nun*, is fit to acquire the higher level of the *vav*, the "crown of Torah."

There is a second aspect of the *ayin's* design, which is that the *ayin* is actually two eyes united at the optical chiasma—the nerve center that receives and interprets visual impulses—at the back of the head. Two eyes attached to a central link can be clearly seen in the letter's form.[2] This offers us a new understanding of the *mitzvah* of donning *tefillin*: specifically to the positioning of the head *tefillin*. In *Deuteronomy*[3] it says that G-d's commandments shall be "between your eyes." In Jewish law, between one's eyes means the point between the eyes as it

---

1 *Berachos* 28a.
2 *The Wisdom in the Hebrew Alphabet, op. cit.,* p. 173.
3 6:8.

travels up just above the hairline. In actuality, the proper position of the head *tefillin* is slightly above the hairline atop the soft part of the skull. Viewed from above, this soft spot is literally at the mid-point between one's eyes[4] and the chiasma. The head *tefillin* is thus set directly between the physical eyes of the body and the eye of the brain, just as the Torah prescribes.

All twenty-two letters of the *alef-beis* may be written in the Torah in small, medium, or large size. Most letters are medium sized, but there are many instances of small and large letters. The first word of the *Shema* שמע is written with a large *ayin*.

In his commentary on the Book of *Psalms,* the Tzemach Tzedek[5] explains that this large *ayin* is in fact the antidote to the *ayin* of the word *miyaar* ("of the forest"), which appears in Psalm 80[6]: "The boar of the forest (*miyaar*) ravages it [the vine of Israel], and the crawler of the field feeds on it." The *ayin* of the word "forest"–מיער–is suspended slightly above the rest of the word. *Rashi* says that if the Jews are righteous and do G-d's will, then this suspended *ayin* will be transformed into the *alef* of the word יאר, *yaar,* meaning "river." A boar in a forest is dangerous. It can attack and seriously harm someone. A boar in a river, however, can't swim. It is rendered harmless.

It is interesting to note that the suspended *ayin* of *miyaar* occurs at the exact mid-point of the Book of *Psalms.*[7] The halfway point of the Torah happens to be the word *gachon,*[8] which is translated as "snake." Both these mid-point terminologies connote evil or doom. The power of Torah, however, is that with it, the meritorious Jew can rend in two the boar of the

---

4 One's eyes are not the actual location of the faculty of sight; rather they are the windows through which light passes.
5 See fn. 1 in chapter on *lamed.*
6 V. 14.
7 *Kiddushin* 30a.
8 *Leviticus* 11:41.

forest and the snake, the forces of evil, signified by the placement of both these words in their respective books.

The *Maharsha*[9] explains that the *ayin* of *miyaar* represents the *ayin* of Esau, עשו, and his descendants, the nation of Amalek, עמלק, who constantly attempt to destroy the Jewish people. It states in *Chassidus* that Esau and Amalek and their descendents attempt to "cool down" the Jews' passionate quest for G-dliness. We refer to the verse[10] which is commonly translated as "[Amalek] struck those of you who were hindmost." In Hebrew, the word translated here as "struck," קרך, actually means "cooled down." The nation of Amalek—whether it exists outside of the Jewish people or within us in the form of the *yetzer hara*, the evil inclination—is that which tells us, "Cool down." Esau, like his brother Jacob, also knows the laws of Torah. But *he* says, "Come on. Don't take the Torah so seriously. You won't be the first one to sin. You won't be the first not to put on *tefillin* or keep Shabbos. Cool down. It's not so important...." Therefore, the *ayin* of the *Shema* is large because the *Shema* expresses our unconditional acceptance of the yoke of G-d. And having made that commitment, the Jew transforms the *ayin* of Esau and Amalek, which is indifference, to the *ayin* of the *Shema*, which is passion for G-dliness.

Gematria

The numerical value of *ayin* is seventy.

In his opening address to the Academy, Rabbi Elazar ben Azaryah said:[11] "I am *like* a seventy-year-old man and I had never succeeded in proving that one has to recite the [verse about] going out of Egypt [in the third paragraph of the *Shema*] at night until I found the words of Ben Zoma, who explained

9 *Kiddushin* 30a.
10 *Deuteronomy* 25:18.
11 *Passover Haggadah*, the third paragraph after the "Four Questions."

the verse 'Remember going out of Egypt all the days of your life' as follows: Why does the verse include the word 'all'? It seems to be redundant. Therefore, Ben Zoma explains, 'The "days of your life" means the daytime. "All" comes to include the nights as well.' The Rabbis add to the words of Ben Zoma, 'The "days of your life" refer to the days of this world, the world in which we're presently living. *All* the days, however, includes the days of *Mashiach*.'"

Now two obvious questions arise. First, why is it important that Rabbi Elazar ben Azaryah said, "I am like seventy" when he delivered his inaugural speech? Secondly, why did he choose to deliver his first public address on the third paragraph of the *Shema*?

Seventy represents one who is in total control of his emotional attributes. As we discussed in the chapter on *kaf*, there are seven general emotional characteristics. Each one of these seven traits in turn contains ten levels: the three of the intellect and the seven of the emotions.[12] When an individual has totally refined all of these seventy levels, he is then fit to lead and teach others. The Rebbe once said, "First you must become a master over yourself, the personal world within. Then you must master your family environment. Only then can you endeavor to be a leader in the world."[13]

At the age of seventy, or "like seventy," after one has acquired the requisite strength and vision and has attained these seventy levels of spirituality, one is then fit to be a *Nasi* in Israel.

What's the job of a leader? To bring redemption to his people. We now see the brilliance of Rabbi Elazar ben Azaryah's first

---

12 The realm of Kabbalah is a complex, interactive matrix: the Ten Attributes, or *Sefiros*, have separate functions but are inclusive of and intertwined with all the other attributes. To cite an example in the body: just as the kidneys are a separate organ, their function and efficacy are dependent upon and connected with the surrounding internal organs.

13 See *Sichas Yud Shevat*, 5735.

address. It was not merely a speech; it was a mission statement,[14] as will be explained below.

Etymologically, the Hebrew word for Egypt, *Mitzrayim*, means "constraints," and "limitations." The job of a *Nasi* is to help his people go forth from these self-imposed or general limitations. This is known as *Geulah*—Redemption—and the days of *Mashiach*. There are three stages to this Redemption:

The first stage is to recite the passage about "going out of Egypt"[15] during the day. This represents the condition of living in light: when times are good, when the Jewish people have their land, and there's no danger of assimilation or anti-Semitism (e.g., the near-perfect state that existed during the period of the First Holy Temple). When things are going well, one is obligated to make even greater strides and thrive: to immerse oneself in prayer and study; to attain even greater levels of piety by helping others; to write commentaries and expound on the teachings of the Torah and *Talmud*.

The second stage, as pertains to Ben Zoma, is to recite *at night* the passage on "the going out of Egypt." For even during exile, even during the darkest and most challenging hours, an individual or a people are required to go out from their current borders. A person must transcend his constraints, regardless of his economic condition or social status. The *Rambam* is a perfect example. He first escaped the Almohads in Spain. He then fled to Morocco and eventually settled in Egypt, the land of "constraints and limitations." What did the *Rambam* do there, in this dark, foreign environment hostile to Jews? He wrote his magnum opus known as the *Mishneh Torah*, the only text in history that codified the entire Torah. The *Rambam* not only transcended his boundaries, he transformed them.

---

14 I.e., "that as your leader, I will bring you to Redemption."
15 In the third passage of the *Shema*.

Finally, the Rabbis say that in this world, even before the ultimate revelation of *Mashiach*, we must incorporate the reality of Redemption into our very being, our constitution. We must live our lives as Jews to the fullest measure. We must go out unconditionally from *all* borders, be they material limitations or those of doubt or fear. A leader motivates his followers to make that leap. The leader within each of us can effect our own individual and personal redemption.

Meaning

Ayin means eyes, as it states:[16] "And your eyes עיניך, *einecha*, shall see your Teacher (i.e., G-d)." Another verse reads: "And the glory of G-d shall be revealed and all flesh shall *see* together that the mouth of G-d speaks."[17] Only one who is "like seventy"—one who has refined each of the seven emotional attributes, as explained above—can reach the level of seeing G-dliness in this world. With this quality of insight, one can lead a nation to Redemption.

Furthermore, *ayin* also stands for salvation, *eizer*, עזר. Rabbi Elazar ben Azaryah's name itself intimates a special salvation from G-d. Elazar (in Hebrew, *E-l eizer*), אלעזר, means "G-d is [my] salvation." Azaryah עזרי-ה means "[My] salvation is G-d." This explains Rabbi Elazar ben Azaryah's statement, "I am like seventy years old." For Rabbi Elazar ben Azaryah had acquired all the qualities needed for leadership because G-d was his help and salvation. He was therefore endowed with this rare quality of leadership at such an early age.

This then is the meaning of being a leader: to visualize—*see*—Redemption and convey this message to others. As such, one

---

16 *Isaiah* 30:20.
17 *Ibid.* 40:5.

thereby transforms the *ayin* of *miyaar* to the *ayin* of the *Shema*—where one can "Lift up [one's] eyes and see G-d."[18]

---

18 *Chassidus* tells us that the word *Shema*, שמע, is an acronym for *S'u marom eineichem* שאו מרום עיניכם—"Lift up your eyes and see G-d" (See *HaYom Yom*, entry for 19 MarCheshvan).

פף
פּי

Pei

PEI—COMMUNICATION

Design	Mouth with a tooth emerging; white space of the *pei* is a *beis*
Gematria	Eighty
Meaning	Mouth

In Israel, a fifteen-year-old girl woke up one morning to discover suddenly that she could no longer speak. After three days of shock and denial, her parents brought her to an elite doctor in Tel Aviv. The physician examined her. Then he told the mother and father, "It is impossible that this girl has ever spoken. She has no vocal chords." The parents protested that their daughter had been speaking for fifteen years! Nevertheless, the doctor proclaimed he could do nothing to help her.

After many months and numerous visits to all the top specialists, the family's last hope was a doctor in England. He too concluded that the girl's case was hopeless. By chance, the family happened to encounter a Chabadnik on their journey. The man advised them to see the Lubavitcher Rebbe.

The father was reluctant, but the mother insisted. She started making phone calls and arranged their trip to the United States. The family went into the Rebbe's office and the mother immediately started to sob uncontrollably. After several minutes she got hold of herself and told the Rebbe their story. The Rebbe asked the parents to leave the room so that he could speak to the girl alone. He said to her, "I know you are an intelligent girl and will appreciate what I have to say. In your previous *gilgul* (incarnation), you did many things that were not very good. What they were isn't important. What *is* important is to know that it was decreed in Heaven that your punishment was to come down to this world and be born mute. However, because you were blessed with great and holy forebears, for their merits you were given fifteen years of speech. From now on you will not be able to speak... *unless* you agree to use your mouth to talk to other children about keeping Shabbos. If you agree to do this, you will once again speak. Do you agree?"

The girl nodded. The Rebbe pressed her for a commitment, "So. We have a deal?" The girl opened her mouth and out came the word "yes." To this day that girl—now a grown woman—gathers children together every Shabbos to speak to them about the sanctity of the day.[1]

Design

The seventeenth letter of the *alef-beis* is the *pei*. The design of the *pei* is a mouth with a tooth emerging from its upper jaw. To understand the significance of this design requires the recounting of a Biblical story and a visual comparison between the letters *pei* and *kaf*. A quick glance shows that the *kaf* closely resembles the *pei*; only the "tooth" in the *pei* is absent from the *kaf*.

In the Book of *Exodus*,[2] Pharaoh, whose name also begins with a *pei*, said, "Let us [confine the Jews to slavery] lest they multiply." The word for "lest" in Hebrew is פן, *pen*: *pei-nun*. G-d was displeased with Pharaoh's declaration, so He "knocked out his tooth" by knocking out the tooth of the *pei* in Pharaoh's "*pen*," which made it a *kaf*. Now the word was no longer *pen* ("lest") but כן, *ken*: *kaf-nun*, meaning "surely." *Surely* the Jews will multiply.[3]

Gematria

The *gematria* of *pei* is eighty. As it says in *Ethics of Our Fathers*:[4] "When one is eighty years old, he has reached a special strength." Therefore we find: "Eighty thousand men by the name of Aaron all followed Aaron to his final resting place."[5] The reason there were eighty thousand men by the name of Aaron is as follows: We know Aaron was a great

---

1 *Kfar Chabad Magazine*, Issue 674, p. 62.
2 1:10.
3 See *Rashi*, *Exodus* 1:12, quoting the *Midrash*. Also see the commentary *Kli Yakar* on *Exodus* 1:8.
4 5:22.
5 *Kallah Rabasi*, ch. 3.

speaker. When G-d asked Moses to speak to Pharaoh, Moses demurred, saying that he had a speech impediment. G-d responded, "Is there not your brother, Aaron the Levite? I know that he can speak well." Aaron's verbal skills also served him well as a marriage counselor. When there was a fight between a couple and the husband or wife left, Aaron became the peacemaker, appeasing them with soothing words. When the reunited couple gave birth to its next child, they invariably said, "We will name the child after Aaron the High Priest." He reunited so many couples that thousands of children were named Aaron. Thus the number eighty (thousand) here signifies the special strength of the *pei*, the mouth.

Moses was eighty years old when he led the Jews out of Egypt and eighty when he transmitted the Torah to them.

Meaning

The letter *pei* actually means "mouth"—*peh*. A mouth is something we use to speak, and the entire purpose of speaking is to communicate with another individual. That ability to communicate is the essential aspect of eighty's special strength.

Speech has tremendous power. A king rules with his words. An ordinary person also has great power in his mouth. With words of praise he can raise a person to great heights, and with a bit of gossip he can destroy a person's reputation.

According to the Baal Shem Tov, everyone has a psalm in the Book of *Psalms*—the one corresponding to his age.[6] If a person is 80 years old, for example, he should say Psalm 81. Psalm 81 states: "I am G-d your L-rd Who lifted you out of Egypt. Widen your mouth and I will fill it." Two questions present themselves here. First, how is one able to "widen" his mouth? The mouth has a certain size. How can one stretch it beyond its natural

---

6 When a person reaches his 80th birthday, for example, he has begun his 81st year of life. Hence, the psalm in the Book of *Psalms* is the person's age plus one.

parameters? Secondly, why does it say, "I am G-d, Who *lifted* you from the land of Egypt?" In the book of *Exodus*[7] it reads, "*Hotzeisicha*—I *took* you out," not, as the psalm states, that "I *lifted* you." So, what is the connection between these two verses? Furthermore, what is the connection between an eighty-year-old person and Psalm 81?[8]

As discussed earlier, the word for Egypt, *Mitzrayim*, connotes restraints or borders, a narrow place. A Jew must realize that every day of his life, G-d not only releases him from the shackles of Egypt ("takes him out"), but gives him the opportunity to break through an even higher and more subtle level of limitation ("lifts him"). G-d gives a Jew the ability to go beyond his personal physical limits and even beyond nature. This is alluded to by the expression "widening our mouths," as explained below.[9]

Recall that the letter *beis*, which begins the Torah, has three sides. Its missing fourth side signifies that the world is incomplete. The Jew, however, has the ability and responsibility to complete G-d's creation, to go beyond what he believes possible and make the world whole. We accomplish this by widening our mouths. With the use of our mouths to praise G-d, learn Torah, pray, and communicate positive messages to others, we complete the world. In this way we fulfill our purpose in coming to this world, by transforming nature and making the world a better place in which to live.

That mission is signified by the number 81. G-d tells us that He lifts us out of Egypt. But not only does He physically raise us from the narrow place, He spurs us to move from 80 to 81. Even though we are 80, the upper limit of our strength, G-d

---

7 20:2.
8 See *Likkutei Sichos*, vol. 10, fn. 31 on pp. 75-76.
9 *Ibid.*, p. 76.

gives us the ability to break that barrier and move one level higher.

One can therefore say that eighty also denotes strength in leadership and character. *Ayin*, as we said in the last chapter, stands for leadership. When you have been a leader for ten years, you have refined all aspects of your leadership skills and can now guide with authority and confidence.

Everyone has the ability to communicate and inspire others. One should not shy away from that responsibility claiming, "I have an impediment." Moses had an impediment, yet he revealed the ability to lead a nation of several million people for forty years. All of us have impediments in one area or another. Yet those external weaknesses should never incapacitate us or stymie our desire to bestow goodness and communicate words of inspiration to others.

G-d told Moses, "*Anochi eheyeh im picha*[10]—I will be your mouthpiece." The word *anochi* has the *gematria* of 81: *alef*=1, *nun*=50, *kaf*=20, *yud*=10. If a person is humble and relies upon G-d to be his mouthpiece, his power of speech will transcend its natural limits and be a source of strength for others.

There is a famous teaching of Rabbi Levi Yitzchak of Berditchev[11] which explains the meaning of the Passover holiday (Pesach). "Pesach" literally means *peh-sach*, "the mouth *(peh)* talks *(sach)*." On Pesach, the mouth talks about the wonders and miracles of G-d. Pesach represents the antithesis of Pharaoh, who, as the *Megaleh Amukos*[12] explains, signifies *peh-ra*, a "bad mouth." Pharaoh was someone who denied G-d's providence in every act of nature. Our mouths were not given to

---

10 *Exodus* 4:12.
11 *Kedushas Levi, Derush LePesach*, p. 61c; see also *Siddur HaAriZal* on Pesach.
12 *Parshas Bo.*

us to slander or denigrate others, but to speak of G-d's greatness and wonders.[13]

---

13 Regarding the final *pei*, one can say that the straight or final *pei* represents extending one's speech; going beyond one's domain to reach out to social arenas that are "beneath the base line," that are antithetical to G-dliness and spirituality, so that the message should reach and inspire them as well. See *Maharsha* on *Shabbos* 104a for a different interpretation of the final *pei*.

צֵן

צ

צריק צדקה

Tzaddik

TZADDIK—THE BAAL TESHUVAH

Design	*Yud* and bent *nun*
Gematria	Ninety
Meaning	Righteous

A man living in California once came to the Lubavitcher Rebbe for *yechidus* (a private audience). He was afflicted with an incurable case of psoriasis and came to ask the Rebbe for help. He told the Rebbe, "I've heard great things about you. I've heard that you perform miracles and I came to ask you to perform a miracle for me. As for my background, I went through the Holocaust. I don't pray to G-d and I don't believe in G-d. But I do believe in *tzaddikim* (completely righteous people). My father was a Bobover chassid and always went to his Rebbe for blessings, so I've always believed in the power of *tzaddikim*."

The Rebbe replied that a *tzaddik* has no power of his own. A *tzaddik* is merely an extension of G-d here in this world to help people, which he does by tapping into G-d's powers. "If you don't believe in G-d, you cannot believe in me."

The man waved his hand, "Eh! I still believe in *tzaddikim*." So the Rebbe told him to take off his shirt and undershirt and stand up. The Rebbe got up from his chair. He took his two hands and put them on the man's right arm and slid them from top to bottom, upon which the psoriasis disappeared. The Rebbe repeated the action with the man's left arm and again the man's scales receded. Then the Rebbe took his two hands and applied them to the man's chest and back. The psoriasis fell away. The Rebbe told his visitor that he normally did not perform revealed miracles. Generally, Heavenly assistance would appear in a more concealed manner. But there are always exceptions to the rule. He hoped that from that day on, the man would once again believe in G-d and begin living a life of Torah and *mitzvos*.[1]

---

1 From the tape series *"Mashiach, the Crown of Creation,"* tape #3. Story told by Rabbi Immanuel Schochet.

Design

Tzaddik is the eighteenth letter of the *alef-beis*.

The design of a *tzaddik* is a *yud* on top of the letter *nun*.[2] One interpretation of the *nun* is that it stands for *ona'ah*, deceit and fraud. By nature, most of us have the misconception that it is the physical world that is the source of ultimate truth and pleasure. But the *yud*, or Divine intellect, is added to the *nun* to teach us that the material world is ephemeral, and not the source of consummate goodness and joy. Therefore there must be something truer and more G-dly upon which to focus. This heightened intention is the essence of the *tzaddik*.

The *Zohar* recounts that when G-d wanted to create the world, every letter of the *alef-beis* came before Him and said, "G-d, create the world with *me*." The *tav* came first, and then the *shin*, and so on. Then the *tzaddik* appeared before G-d and said, "G-d, create the world with *me*. I am the *tzaddik*, the righteous one." So G-d responded, "Yes, but because you are righteous you must be hidden. Therefore, I cannot create the world with you."

Chassidus asks why this is so. If the *tzaddik* is righteous, why wouldn't G-d have wanted to use it to create the world? Every creature in the world would then be upright and pure. Rather than living in a realm of immorality, theft and deceit, we would live in a world that is safe, peaceful and G-dly. What would be wrong with that?

The answer is that it would be too easy. G-d's intention is that we should be born into an incomplete physical world and strive to perfect it. With the G-dliness that flows from the *yud*, we can strengthen our ability to overcome the *nun*, the pleasures of the corporeal world. The *tzaddik* must therefore be concealed in Creation so that one strives for righteousness on his own.

2 *Zohar* III, p. 180b; *Sefer HaArachim Chabad, Osios*, letter *tzaddik*, p. 315.

Gematria

The numerical equivalent of the letter *tzaddik* is ninety. In *Ethics of Our Fathers*[3] it says: "When one reaches the age of ninety, one is bent over (*lashuach*)." On a physical level, this means that at ninety, a man is infirm and bowed with weakness. On a spiritual plane, it represents the concept of humility. When one reaches ninety, he has become so spiritual and humble that he bends over for G-d. He is no longer an independent character but an extension of G-d Himself.

At the age of ninety, one has achieved a heightened level of prayer. He has the ability to feel a direct connection to G-d when he prays. Additionally, it is explained in the *Midrash Shmuel*[4] that the word *lashuach* means "to pray constantly." That connection is the foundation of a *tzaddik*. A *tzaddik* exists not for his own benefit, but to serve as an offshoot of G-d. We go to *tzaddikim* to pray on our behalf because we know that the prayers of the *tzaddik* will be answered.[5]

Meaning

The name *tzaddik* means "righteous one," a leader and teacher of a generation. We also know that many *tzaddikim* are called Rebbe. This tradition began with Moses, the first Rebbe of the Jewish people. Another famous *tzaddik* known as "Rebbe" is Rabbi Yehudah HaNasi, the redactor of the *Mishnah*. There is a Rebbe in every generation, a *tzaddik* who is that era's spiritual leader.

What is the concept of a Rebbe? "Rebbe," רבי, is an acronym for *Rosh B'nei Yisrael*, "the head of the Jewish people."[6] What is

---

3 5:22, according to *Rashi's* commentary on the *mishnah*.

4 *Ibid.*

5 Even though one prays directly to G-d, one's prayers can sometimes be rejected due to one's sins and ego. But the prayers of a *tzaddik*, which are refined and untainted, can pierce through all the heavenly gates.

6 *Degel Machne Ephraim, Parshas Yisro*; also see *Sefer HaMaamarim 5710*, p. 254; *Toras Menachem 5713*, vol. III, p. 144.

a head? The head of a body is its control center. It gives life, nourishment, and direction to the rest of the body. It also feels the pain, desires and needs of every aspect of its body.

A Rebbe, then, is both literally and figuratively the head of the Jewish community. When a person has a dilemma, what should he or she do? Perhaps the problem is whether or not to visit Israel, buy a house, or marry a certain man or woman. That person goes to visit the Rebbe. Just as the head houses the eyes, the Rebbe is the eyes of his community. He has the ability to see things that the lone questioning individual cannot.[7]

A Rebbe's ability to intervene on behalf of the Jewish people is not magic. It is a natural and organic outgrowth of his righteousness. Just as it is perfectly normal for the head to feel and respond to the needs of the whole body, it is natural for the Rebbe to feel and respond to the needs of his people.

What sources support the premise that a Jew can get closer to G-d through communication with a Rebbe? Moreover, doesn't Judaism frown on "intermediaries" between man and G-d? The answer lies in the *mitzvah u'ledavka bo*,[8] which means to cleave to G-d. The *Rambam*,[9] based on the words of the *Talmud*, asks, "How is it possible that one should cleave to G-d? G-d is fire and we are physical. One who touches fire will burn." The Sages answer, "'To cleave unto Him' means that we should cleave to wise men and to their disciples," i.e., *tzaddikim*. We cleave through connection with a *tzaddik*, who is one with G-d. Furthermore, believing in *tzaddikim* is based on a verse in *Exodus* said every day in our morning prayers:[10] "[The Jews]

---

7 Rabbi Joseph B. Soloveitchik (1903-1993) said in the name of Rabbi Yisrael Salanter (1810-1883), "Even *misnagdim* (non-Chassidic Jews) need a Rebbe; however, the problem with the *misnagdim* is that they are too critical, and as a result do not find one (*The Rav*, vol. 1, p. 159, *op. cit.*).

8 *Deuteronomy* 11:22.

9 Positive Commandment #6.

10 *Siddur Tehillat Hashem*, p. 39, 164.

believed in G-d and Moses His servant."[11] The *Mechilta*[12] queries, "Why is it important to tell us that the Jewish people believed in Moses His servant? How can we equate our faith in Moses with our belief in G-d?" The answer is, without faith in Moses, or the Moses of every generation, there cannot be belief in G-d.

G-d puts *tzaddikim* in this world to testify to the fact that He exists.[13] By virtue of our connection to these righteous people and our belief in them, we are provided with a channel to connect with G-d.

The letter *tzaddik* has two forms. There is the bent *tzaddik* which occurs at the beginning or middle of a word. Then there is the straight *tzaddik* which occurs at the end of a word. What is the significance of each? The straight *tzaddik* represents the *baal teshuvah*, one who has worked to improve his connection to G-d and returned to his essential holy nature. The bent *tzaddik* is born righteous, but has not yet reached the level of a *baal teshuvah*. As we are told, even a complete *tzaddik* cannot stand in the place of a *baal teshuvah*.[14] A *baal teshuvah* stands higher.

What does this mean? How is it possible that a *baal teshuvah*—one who has sinned all his life and then decides to change—stands higher than a *tzaddik*? There are two reasons. The first is that the one who has transgressed has already tasted cheeseburgers and lobster, and relished them. Now he must wrest himself from their grip. It is similar to the difficulty experienced by a long-time smoker who now wants to quit. There might be a certain temptation on the part of one who has never smoked to try a cigarette. But having never smoked, it is much easier for him to control the temptation. One who has

11 *Exodus* 14:31.
12 On the above verse.
13 See *Sefer Halkarim*, book 3, chs. 8, 12.
14 *Rambam's Code of Jewish Law: Laws of Teshuvah* 7:4.

already experienced its physical pleasure, however, might be hooked. It is very difficult to extirpate that aspect from his life, and it requires tremendous strength and commitment. Thus a *baal teshuvah* who was born to a non-religious home, who never learned anything about Judaism, and lives according to the secular ways of the world creates an elevated connection to G-d when he decides to change. G-d says, "You, My dear child, stand higher than the *tzaddik*."

The second reason the *baal teshuvah* stands higher than the *tzaddik* is that the wrongdoings of the *baal teshuvah* are converted into *mitzvos*. Once his past sins have been renounced, they are actually credited as positive commandments.[15]

How is this possible? The answer to that question requires a discussion of the method by which neutral and impure entities are spiritually elevated. There are two arenas in the physical world: the realm of the neutral and the realm of the impure. The realm of the neutral contains things that are capable of being elevated to holiness, like kosher food, Shabbos candles, and an *esrog* (citron) for the *lulav*. Those things that are completely impure (i.e., pork, forbidden relationships) cannot be elevated and are therefore prohibited.

As an example of how the neutral realm can be affected, let's say that I take an apple or a piece of kosher chicken and make a blessing on it before eating it. What's my ultimate purpose in eating? Not to satisfy or gratify my selfish personal needs, but to acquire the strength to serve G-d. Making a blessing before one eats empowers the individual to elevate the food. In so doing, the neutral realm of the food has been elevated to the level of spirituality.

---

15 There are three basic ways to acquire merit through the commandments: The first comprises the 248 positive, or active, commandments (i.e., doing something that has been commanded). The second includes the 365 negative, or passive, commandments (i.e., refraining from doing something prohibited). The third is the transformation of a negative commandment into a positive one (through the process of *teshuvah* or repentance).

Conversely, consider the fact that I'm eating simply because I'm ravenous. I just want to fill my stomach, and G-d is the last thing on my mind. In this instance, I'm taking the neutral arena and drawing it down into the three levels of impurity. This arena of impurity denotes not only that which is prohibited— pork, shrimp, non-kosher meat and so forth—but that which is neutral and debased through improper action or intention.

Now, how do I elevate that which is impure by nature—that which is unable to be elevated under normal circumstances? By *resisting* it. For example, you're walking down the street and see a hot dog stand. You have a desire to eat a hot dog even though they are not kosher. The moment you say, "No, I won't eat one," you've performed a *mitzvah*. You get credit for a *mitzvah* by *not* eating it, by curbing your desire. This is the meaning of fulfilling a negative commandment. Nevertheless, while the credit for fulfilling a negative (passive) commandment is similar to performing a positive (active) one, it is not quite identical.[16]

Now, to return to the original question, let's say you've transgressed a negative commandment (e.g., done or eaten something prohibited). How do you transform the penalties associated with violating a negative commandment into the rewards generated by performance of a positive commandment? This is accomplished by the decision to do *teshuvah*. You say, "G-d, I'm sorry for the past. I want to return to You. I will never sin again." At that moment, all the accumulated sins become positive commandments.[17]

16 Resisting a negative commandment is considered "as if" you've done a positive commandment, whereas doing *teshuvah* (i.e., regretting something you did wrong and resolving not to do it again) is considered an actual positive commandment. See *Kiddushin* 39b; *Makkos* 23b. See also *Likkutei Sichos*, vol. 1, p. 203.

17 *Yoma* 86b.

It is interesting to note that while resisting something prohibited gives the *person* credit for a positive *mitzvah*, there is a way that completely impure *things* can be elevated to holiness: Let's say a non-observant youngster had a weakness for ham sandwiches. Years

Perhaps by knowing this someone could say, "Great. Now I can go down to the hot dog stand, eat a few frankfurters, and make up for it by doing *teshuvah* later." Unfortunately it doesn't work that way. Anyone who says, "I will intentionally sin and then return to G-d later" is not given the opportunity to repent.[18] A person can't engage in the *teshuvah* process in a deceptive, self-serving manner. The essence of the *baal teshuvah's* return is the pure desire to rectify a previous wrong and return to his intrinsic connection to G-d. Can the one who sins in the present with the idea that he'll repent later, in fact repent? If he is stubborn, yes. Nothing can stand in the way of *teshuvah*, and even for the worst sins in the Torah a person can repent. But in general, if one sins in order to repent, he will not be given the opportunity to do *teshuvah*.

It states in the *Zohar*[19] that when *Mashiach* comes to the world, he will cause all the *tzaddikim* to do *teshuvah*. This means that *Mashiach* will bring a heightened awareness even to that person who has served G-d perfectly every day of his life. This is the bent *tzaddik*. This *tzaddik* will be blessed with an even greater desire and urgency to perform *mitzvos* than he previously possessed. He will have the ability to go beyond his nature and do more than he did yesterday. Thus the bent *tzaddik* will also acquire the qualities of the *baal teshuvah*, the straight *tzaddik*.

When a child is born, he is administered an oath, "Be a *tzaddik* and do not be wicked."[20] From birth, every individual has

later, when he did *teshuvah*, the ham, having become part of his body, became elevated along with the rest of him in the *teshuvah* process. In this way, something completely impure was able to be elevated. A *tzaddik*, on the other hand, would never even think of going near unkosher food, let alone indulge in it. So a *baal teshuvah* can actually elevate more elements of creation than the *tzaddik*. This of course does not give one license to say, "I will sin and then do *teshuvah*," as is explained in the following paragraph.

18 *Ibid.* 85b.
19 III, p. 153b.
20 *Niddah* 30b.

the ability to become a *tzaddik*.[21] If one constantly recalls the existence of this oath, he or she can undoubtedly bring it from potential into reality.

---

21 *Sefer HaSichos 5751*, vol. 2, p. 533, *Parshas Emor*. See translation in *Sichos in English*, vol. 48, p. 159, where it states: "One might object and point out that in *Tanya* itself it is written that not every individual can necessarily become a *tzaddik*, and that one does not have complete free choice in this area. However, since a Jew has the essence of G-d within him, ultimately even this is within his reach. Furthermore, after all the purification, etc., of the Jewish people over the course of time, now every Jew is able to reach the level of *tzaddik*—similar to the way things will be in the Messianic Age.

Kuf

KUF—THE MONKEY

Design	A *hei* with the left foot dipping beneath the line of morality
Gematria	One hundred
Meaning	Monkey

The Rebbe, Rabbi Shmuel of Lubavitch, called for his *shamesh*,[1] Ben-Zion, and asked him: "Have you eaten today?"

"Yes," he answered. "I have eaten."

"Did you eat well?"

"Well? I am satisfied, thank G-d."

"And for what reason did you eat?"

"In order to live."

"And for what reason do you live?"

"So that I can be a proper Jew and do what G-d wants me to do." And then he sighed.

"Please send me Ivan," the Rebbe concluded.

When the wagon driver appeared, the Rebbe asked him: "Have you eaten today?"

"Yes," he answered.

"Did you eat well?"

"Yes."

"And for what reason do you eat?"

"So I can live."

"And for what reason do you live?"

"So I can have a swig of whiskey and fill my stomach."

When Ivan had gone, the Rebbe turned to his children: "You see, then, that Ben-Zion eats in order to live, and lives in order to be a proper Jew and do what G-d commands him to do. Not only that, but he lets out a sigh, too, because he feels that perhaps he is not yet serving G-d as truthfully as he could. As for Ivan, he lives for the sake of his whiskey and his food. Not only that, but he smirks, too, because he's picturing the pleasure he gets out of eating and drinking, and it is for the sake of that pleasure that he lives."[2]

---

1 An attendant.

2 *Kovetz Michtavim*, published with *Sefer Tehillim, Ohel Yosef Yitzchak*, Kehot Publication Society, Brooklyn, NY. Letter dated the 15th of Teves, 5703, pp. 216-218.

Design

The nineteenth letter of the *alef-beis* is the *kuf.*

The design of the *kuf* is similar to that of the *hei*. But while the *hei* represents holiness, the *kuf* represents *kelipah,* or unholiness. Both have three lines, two vertical and one horizontal. These three lines, depicting thought, speech and action in the *hei*, are also represented in the letter *kuf,* but its three lines represent unholy thoughts, profane speech and evil actions. These negative qualities are illustrated within the actual form of the *kuf.* Its long left leg plunges beneath the letter's baseline. It represents one who ventures below the acceptable, an individual who violates the circumscribed boundaries of the Torah.

It is also significant that the head of the *kuf* is a *reish* (in contrast with the *dalet* that comprises the *hei*). We said previously that the difference between the *dalet* and the *reish* is the *yud* in the right-hand corner of the *dalet,* representing G-dliness. Given this, the difference between the holiness of the *hei* and the unholiness of the *kuf* is even more pronounced.

The *Zohar* calls the *kuf* and the *reish* the letters of falsehood and impurity. We observe this by combining the *kuf* and the *reish*, forming the word *kar,* קַר, which means "cold." Coldness represents unholiness and death. It is antithetical to the state of warmth, life and passion. Who is alive? "Every one of you who has cleaved to G-d your L-rd is alive today." [3] One who is connected to G-d every moment of his life is perpetually warm and alive. On the other hand, coldness signifies an abyss—the severance of the connection between man and G-d—and ultimate death.

Now reverse the *kuf* and the *reish* and it spells the word *reik,* רֵק. *Reik* means "empty." As we read in the portion of *Vayei-*

---

3 *Deuteronomy* 4:4.

shev:[4] "The pit was empty (*reik*); there was no water." *Rashi* explains that there were snakes and scorpions in the pit. Why would we assume that the pit contained snakes and scorpions if the Torah does not mention it explicitly? *Rashi* answers with a question: "Isn't it obvious that if the pit is empty there's no water there? The fact that the Torah says there was no water must come to teach us that there were snakes and scorpions." We are told that Torah is synonymous with water. Without Torah, there is only poison and doom.

Gematria

The *gematria* of *kuf* is one hundred. In this, too, we find the concept of death. The *Talmud*[5] tells of a time when one hundred of King David's soldiers would perish daily from an epidemic. David beseeched G-d for help. G-d's reply was to institute the recital of one hundred blessings a day, which David enacted to counteract the one hundred deaths. The one hundred blessings are hinted at in the verse: "What (*mah*) does G-d ask of you?"[6] The word *mah*, "what," can also be read as *meah*, which literally means "one hundred." What does G-d ask of you? Only to recite one hundred blessings daily. And how do we accumulate these one hundred blessings? One recites the *Shemoneh Esreh* (the *Amidah*) three times a day, which contains nineteen blessings each for a total of fifty-seven. In the morning prayers, there are an additional twenty-six blessings. *Maariv*, the evening service, contains four more. Saying the "Grace After Meals" also has four blessings, plus two when we wash our hands and make a blessing on bread. It is thus quite easy to reach one hundred blessings in a day. The *kuf*, one hundred, represents death. But

4 *Genesis* 37:24.
5 *Menachos* 43b; *Shulchan Aruch of the Alter Rebbe*, vol. I, ch. 46:1.
6 *Deuteronomy* 10:12.

if one recites these one hundred blessings daily, one can transform a negative decree into a celebration of life.

Meaning

The name *kuf* in Hebrew means monkey. What is a monkey? A mimic, as in the well-known adage: "Monkey see, monkey do." The letter *kuf* is also a mimic. It imitates the letter *hei*. It is the *kuf's* extended left leg and the *reish* for its head that create the difference between life (*hei*) and death.

Recalling the story in the *Zohar*, each letter of the *alef-beis* approached G-d when He created the world, saying, "G-d, create the world with *me*." When the *shin* appeared before G-d, He said, "I cannot create the world with you, for you spell the word שקר, *sheker* (falsehood)." Even though the letter *shin* is holy, the fact that it is united here with the *kuf* and the *reish* taints its holiness. The world could thus not be created with the letter *shin*. But if the *kuf* and the *reish* by themselves signify falsehood and impurity, why did they need the *shin*? Because the *shin* is the letter of truth. And if falsehood does not attach itself in some way to truth, it cannot stand. Without it, a lie simply becomes ridiculous. Therefore the *kuf* and the *reish* must incorporate the *shin*, the letter of truth, to form a viable and convincing falsehood.

It is man's responsibility to transform the word *sheker*, שקר, into the word *keresh*. *Keresh*, קרש, is composed of the same three letters, but it means a "board." When the Jews were in the desert, they used *kerashim* (boards) to construct the *Mishkan*, or house of G-d. The Torah tells us that these boards were fashioned from *atzei shitim*, acacia wood. The commentators ask, "How is it possible that this Jewish nation, in flight from Egypt, should find acacia wood in the middle of the desert?" The answer is that Jacob our Forefather saw through Divine inspiration that the Jews would need the acacia wood. He planted these trees when he went down to Egypt 210 years before. So why acacia wood? Why not oak, or pine?

The word *shitim* (acacia) in Hebrew means *shtus*, folly. It states in the *Talmud* that one does not sin unless a spirit of folly has entered him.[7] In other words, a Jew by nature neither wants nor can sever his relationship with G-d. It is only the spirit of folly that makes him do so. Such a person may say, "Who cares about a bunch of silly rules? What does G-d care if I light Shabbos candles or not? What difference does it make if I keep kosher or put on *tefillin*? It has no bearing on my life." Due to this irrational way of thinking, a person will come to sin.

The antithesis of irrational thinking which leads to sin is suprarational thinking which can lead to great and praiseworthy accomplishments. As the *Talmud*[8] relates, there was once a Sage, Reb Shmuel bar Rav Yitzchak, who would juggle three myrtle branches before a bride to perform the *mitzvah* of bringing joy to a bride and groom. The other Sages made fun of him. "How can you do such a thing? You're a holy Sage. You embarrass us." When this great Sage died, a pillar of fire shot from his grave all the way to Heaven. His colleagues concluded that he merited this bolt of light due to his "folly in the realm of holiness."

The same concept holds true with regard to the *Mishkan*. The folly of this world must be transformed into a folly that is suprarational. One must be willing to serve G-d beyond his comfort zone and rationality.

This is reflected in the transposition of the letters of *sheker*, שקר, into the word *keresh*, קרש. By acting against the currents of the world's standards and devoting oneself to purifying the material world, one transforms falsehood (*sheker*) into the

---

7 *Sotah* 3a; *Tanya*, ch. 24. Also see the *maamar Basi LeGani*, ch. 3, (in translation, Kehot Publication Society, Brooklyn, NY, 1990).

8 *Kesubos* 17a.

upright beams of acacia wood (*keresh*) that form the Sanctuary. Through this, one brings G-dliness down from the heavens and fashions a home for G-d here on earth.

We can also relate this transformation to the holiday of Chanukah. It states in the *Talmud*[9] that one is to light the Chanukah candles when it gets dark. Until what time may one light the candles? The *Talmud* says, "Until there are no longer 'feet' walking in the marketplace." The concept of the foot, or leg, is relevant to the letter *kuf.* What do we find in the marketplace? A cavalcade of feet. Remember that the foot of the *kuf* extends beneath the baseline; it sinks below the level of Torah. Indeed, a marketplace is a place of chaos, an environment where G-d is barely known. In a place of falsehood, the act of lighting candles can obliterate the darkness and instead fill the area with light and joy. By lighting the Chanukah candles at the prescribed time, we thus help elevate the feet that have fallen below the line to the level of holiness. We transform the negativity of debased thought, speech and action into behavior that will submit to and embrace His law.

Thus, on one hand, the *kuf* represents death and negative thought, speech and action. On the other hand, it invites transformation. Just as the design of the three-sided *beis* embodies a certain tension that is resolved in the four-sided *mem*, so does the foot of the *kuf* call out to be elevated from its station below the horizon. We all have the ability to transform the irrational to the superrational, thus directing our thought, our speech, and our action solely toward G-d and holiness.

9 *Shabbos* 21b.

ר

רֹאשׁ

רֹאשׁ   ראש השנה

Reish

REISH—EVIL

Design	Bent over, lacks the *yud* of the *dalet*
Gematria	Two hundred
Meaning	1. Poor 2. evil 3. head

The *Ramban* (Rabbi Moshe ben Nachman)[1] had a student, Reb Avner, who unfortunately converted to Christianity and became a high official in the court of Spain.[2]

When the *Ramban* questioned his actions, Avner replied: "I left Judaism because of you.... You taught us that all the laws of Torah, science, and history are hinted to in the Torah portion of *Haazinu*[3]... and I refused to believe this. How could one small portion be so replete with knowledge? Your statement eventually brought me to deny the entire Torah."

The *Ramban* persisted: "What I said is true. If you want, you may challenge me." Avner then asked the *Ramban* to show him where his name, "Avner," appears in *Haazinu*.

G-d endowed the *Ramban* with Divine wisdom, and he quoted the following verse from *Haazinu*[4]:

"אמרתי אפאיהם אשביתה מאנוש זכרם" – I said I would make an end of them. I would cause their memory to vanish from among mankind." The *Ramban* instructed his former student to join the third letters of each of the last four words of the verse to spell the name Avner.

Avner realized his teacher was right and asked the *Ramban* if he could do *teshuvah* for his sins. The *Ramban* replied, "Your repentance lies in the very verse I just quoted." Reb Avner then took a boat and set off on the seas unaccompanied by a sailor or navigator. He was never heard of again.

The Rebbe explains[5] that the third letter of the *first* word of the quoted verse is the letter *reish*, ר, which stands for Reb (or Rabbi). What is most intriguing about this story is that Avner's name, as it is hinted to in the Torah, includes the honorable title

1 (1194-1270) Barcelona, Spain.

2 *Seder HaDoros*, p. 214; see also *Emek HaMelech, Shaar Rishon*, ch. 4.

3 *Deuteronomy*, ch. 32, comprised of only 52 verses.

4 *Ibid.*, 32:26.

5 *Toras Menachem 5742*, vol. 1, p. 109.

of Reb, which he merited through his repentance. In truth,
concludes the Rebbe, even before repenting, he carried the title
of Reb.

Design

The twentieth letter of the *alef-beis* is the letter *reish*. The design
of the *reish* represents an individual who is bent over; a poor
person. The *reish* is composed of two lines, one horizontal and
one vertical. It looks very similar to the *dalet*, but the *dalet* has
a *yud* at its upper right-hand corner, which the *reish* lacks.[6] As
we explained in the chapter on *dalet*, the *yud* represents one
who is subservient to G-d and adheres to every letter of the law.
The *reish's* two lines represent intellect and speech.[7] Because
they are not joined with a *yud*, the speech and intellect of this
individual are for his own gratification—they can even
degenerate and become corrupt and evil. Such a person's
thoughts and speech are often directed to hurting and conspir-
ing against others. In this way he drags his most essential faculties into the depths of unholiness.

The absence of the *yud* is important in another way. The *yud*
signifies *Olam HaBa*, the World to Come. The *Talmud*[8] tells us
that G-d created the physical world with the letter *hei*, and He
created the World to Come, with the letter *yud*. The *yud* thus
represents the judgment that will take place in the World to
Come. A *dalet* is someone who always has in mind that there
will be a Day of Judgment. He is therefore careful about what
he thinks and does. A *reish*, however, is a person who does not
care what he does. He has no regard for his thoughts or speech
because he doesn't believe in the ultimate Day of Judgment
signified by the *yud*.

6 However, this does not exclude the *yud* on the left side of the *reish*, the *yud* or beginning
point that every letter possesses.

7 See chapter on the letter *hei*.

8 *Menachos* 29b.

So the *reish* is the unholy counterpart of the *dalet*.[9] If a *reish* is substituted for the *dalet* in the word *echad*, אחד, the word becomes *acher*, other. The mere removal of the *dalet*'s *yud* changes the concept of "one G-d" to "other gods," or idol worship. By removing the *yud*, thus declaring one's belief in other gods, the *Midrash* tells us it is as if one is "destroying worlds."

We find a reverse situation in regard to the birth of Joseph (Yosef). When Joseph was born, his mother, our Matriarch Rachel, said, "*Yosef li Hashem ben acher*–G-d, add to me another son (*ben*)." In Hebrew, the word *yosef* means "to add." *Acher* means "other." The Tzemach Tzedek explains that the mission of every Jew is to change a person who is "other," who doesn't appreciate holiness, into one who is a *ben* (a child of G-d). In other words we must transform an *acher* into an *echad*, a person who is one with G-d.

Gematria

The numerical equivalent of *reish* is two hundred. It states in the *Talmud* that a poor person is permitted to collect charity from a synagogue if he does not possess two hundred *zuz*.[10] The moment the person has two hundred *zuz*, he is no longer considered to be poor.

Meaning

The word *reish* stands for *rash*, one who is poor. This meaning is illustrated in the famous story of King David[11] after he married Bat Sheva. Bat Sheva had been the wife of one of King David's soldiers whom he had sent to the front lines of battle and who subsequently died. Nathan the Prophet came to David and reproved him with a parable: "There were two men in one

---

9 See chapter on the letter *dalet*.
10 *Peah* 8:8.
11 *II Samuel* 12:1-3.

city; one rich and the other poor. The rich man had many flocks
and herds but the poor man had nothing save one lamb.... The
rich man took the poor man's lamb...." The Hebrew used for the
passage "and the poor man had nothing" is "*v'larash ein kol....*"
So *reish/rash* signifies poverty.

The poverty of the *reish* is more wretched than the destitution
of the *dalet,* a *dal*—who also is a poor person. The poor person
represented by the *dalet* has a pittance, but the *rash* has
nothing.

The *Talmud* states: "There is no poor person except he who is
poor in knowledge."[12] The *reish* is far away from G-d. He enter-
tains flagrant, evil thoughts and speaks negatively. He is beyond the level of having or not having money. He is *spiritually*
bereft; the poorest of the poor.

The *Talmud*[13] tells us that the *reish* also stands for the word
rasha, which means an evil person. We know, however, that
when a wicked person repents, he becomes a *baal teshuvah,* and
is therefore higher than a *tzaddik.* In such a case, the *reish* no
longer means *rasha,* but *rosh,* or "head." This concept is also
hinted in its design and *gematria,* as will be explained.

If you continue drawing the rounded line of the *reish* (ר), it
turns into a *kaf* (כ), representing the *Sefirah* of *Kesser* (crown).[14]
In so doing, the *reish* is elevated to the level of *Kesser.* This is
hinted to by the fact that the *reish* also stands for *rosh* (head)[15]
and the head's skull is considered its crown. Furthermore, the
numerical equivalent of *reish* (200) is 10 times *kaf* (*Kesser*) (20).

The *reish,* at times poor and at times wicked, has the ability
to do *teshuvah.* It can awake from its slumber and repent. The
reish can truly be transformed into the *rosh*: the head of the
Jewish people.

12 *Nedarim* 41a.
13 *Shabbos* 104a.
14 See chapter on the letter *kaf.*
15 *Sefer HaArachim Chabad, Osios,* letter *reish,* p. 376.

שׁ שׂ שׁ

שׁוֹפָר שַׁבָּת שִׁיר

Shin

SHIN—THE MATRIARCHS

Design	Three or four vertical lines; four types of *shin*: 1. *shin* 2. *sin* 3. silent 4. four lines on *tefillin*
Gematria	Three hundred
Meaning	1. Teeth 2. steadfast 3. change 4. return 5. year

Rabbi Shalom Dov Ber Schneersohn, the fifth Rebbe of Lubavitch, wrote a letter to his followers in 1901 that pronounced the 19th of Kislev as the "New Year of *Chassidus.*"[1] When the letter reached the Rebbe's chassidim in the town of Brisk, the 19th of Kislev had already passed. The chassidim wanted to make a special celebration in honor of the Rosh Hashanah of *Chassidus* and planned to do so on Purim Katan (the 14th of Adar I). When word reached the Rav of Brisk, Reb Chaim Brisker,[2] that they were celebrating the 19th of Kislev on Purim Katan, he declared, "We don't mix one joyous day with another. Each holiday requires a day of its own."

When a copy of that same letter reached the chassidim in Vilna, it somehow found its way to the court of Rabbi Chaim Ozer Grodzinsky.[3] Upon seeing it, one of the Rav's fellow judges on the Rabbinical Court scoffed, "The *Mishnah* says there are only four Rosh Hashanahs and they are making a fifth!" Rabbi Chaim Ozer replied, "*You* diminish in holidays. They *add* in holidays!"[4] Rabbi Chaim Ozer's remark implied that the judge was not doing enough to give honor to the holy days that already existed. The Lubavitchers, meanwhile, were willing to do even *more* than what was prescribed.

---

1 The day the Alter Rebbe was released from prison in 1798. See *HaYom Yom*, entry for 19 Kislev.

2 Rabbi Chaim "Brisker" Soloveitchik (1853-1918).

3 Reb Chaim Ozer was a member of the Lithuanian movement and had great respect for chassidim, as they had for him. He was a friend and colleague of the Rebbe Rashab, the fifth Rebbe of *Chabad*, and they worked together on many projects for the Jewish people in Russia.

4 As the story goes, Rabbi Chaim Ozer was referring to the fact that his colleague did not fast on *BeHaB*—the tradition of fasting on Monday, Thursday and Monday after the three major holidays—or the day before the new month. (See the introduction to the Hebrew edition of *Kuntres U'Maayon*, a well-known discourse written by Rabbi Shalom Dov Ber Schneersohn, the Rebbe Rashab, Kehot Publication Society.)

Both stories illustrate that the 19th of Kislev was accepted not only by chassidim but by leading non-Chassidic circles as well.

Design

The twenty-first letter of the *alef-beis* is the *shin*.

The *shin* comprises three vertical lines representing three columns. The letter itself looks like a crown.

The three lines of the *shin* may be interpreted as three general dimensions of a human being: *Kesser* (will and pleasure), the intellect, and the emotions.[5] In addition, the entire *shin* can represent just one of these dimensions, with each of the three lines symbolizing a subdivision of that dimension. In the case of *Kesser, Kesser* is that which exists *beyond* the intellect—the dimension of the suprarational; the will and pleasure of the King. The *gematria* of *Kesser* is 620. When the *shin* is represented as *Kesser*, 620 rays of light are imparted to the world through the three literal lines—or channels—of the *shin*. These rays are bestowed on the world through the right line, which is kindness; the left line, which is justice; and the centerline, mercy.

When the *shin* is representative of the intellectual dimension, the three lines stand for the three intellectual faculties of the *Sefiros*: the right line being *Chochmah*, the flash of an idea; the left line being *Binah*, understanding; and the centerline *Daas*, application of knowledge.

Finally, there is the dimension of the emotions, or *middos*. Here the *shin's* right line represents *Chessed*, kindness; the left line represents *Gevurah*, severity or discipline; and the centerline represents *Tiferes*, mercy or compassion.

---

5 See chapter on the letter *kaf*.

Furthermore, the three lines of the *shin* can signify the three pillars upon which the world stands:[6] the study of Torah, prayer and good deeds.

Yet another dimension of the *shin's* columns is reflected by the three Patriarchs. Abraham is represented by the right line, *Chessed* (loving-kindness), as he personified absolute kindness, an outward focus through connection to others, and the performance of good deeds. Isaac is represented by the left line, *Gevurah* (discipline and severity), indicative of his being introspective and demanding of himself; concentrating on self-refinement and intense prayer. Jacob is the centerline. This is *Tiferes*, or harmony, because he took the qualities of Abraham and Isaac, kindness and severity, and synthesized them into mercy. Jacob also represents Torah study, because the Torah blends the positive and negative commandments into a harmonious whole.

The letter *shin* actually has four different forms. There's a *shin* with a dot above the right column, a *shin* with a dot above the left column, a *shin* with four columns instead of three, and finally a silent *shin*. When the dot is on the right, the *shin* emphasizes *Chessed*, the concept of kindness. When the dot is on the left, the *shin* (pronounced "*sin*") emphasizes the aspect of judgment or severity. These two forms are illustrated by the words *shaar* and *sei'ar*. The *shin* of the word *shaar* (gate) has its point on the right, שער, as a gate allows people to pass in and out, an aspect of openness or *chessed*. This *shin* is full of energy, potential and benevolence.

If we switch the *shin's* dot to the left side, which is *Gevurah* (i.e., contraction), the resulting word is *sei'ar*, שער, or hair. Hair has the properties of life, but a life-force that is tremendously diminished or weak. One can pull out or cut a strand of hair and not feel any pain, unlike when one cuts a finger or other

6 *Ethics of Our Fathers* 1:2.

part of the body. A hair is rooted in a follicle, a concentrated, restricted opening. We thus say that the *shin* with a point on the left side represents severity and constraint.

The *shin* with four columns is found on the *tefillin* that is worn on the head. One side of the head *tefillin* has a *shin* with three lines and the other has one with four lines. In his personal notes[7] the Rebbe offers two reasons for this. First, the four-lined *shin* is the *shin* of the *Luchos*, the Tablets of the Ten Commandments. The four lines represent the awesomeness and holiness of the engraving of G-d's word into physical stone. To visualize this, imagine the three lines of the *shin* etched into stone. If you focus on the stone that remains around the *shin*, there will be four columns. These are the four lines of this form of the *shin*. They are the wake, the reflected light of the *Luchos*.

The second of the Rebbe's reasons is that the four-pronged *shin* represents the four mothers: Sarah, Rebecca, Rachel and Leah.

One can make a connection between these two interpretations. Like the *Luchos*, the teachings of our mothers are truly inscribed upon our hearts and minds. A mother teaches out of love and compassion. Her lessons commence even before birth and make an everlasting impression upon her children. Contrast this with the instruction of one's father. This begins slightly later in life, and often in an atmosphere of austerity and severity.

The mother's education is more fundamental, more indelible and is therefore represented by the *Luchos*, which are engraved. The father's education is likened to the letters of the Torah, ink on parchment, which can be erased. Even though the father's instructions are important, the mother has a more impressionable and permanent effect on the child. Our mothers and the

---

7 *Reshimos* #157, p. 9.

awesomeness of their teachings are therefore, like the *Luchos*, represented by the four-pronged *shin*.

The last of the four forms is the silent *shin*. The silent *shin* is found in the name Yissachar, which contains two *shins*, יששכר. Only the first one is pronounced. What happened to the second? We must first understand who Yissachar was. Yissachar and Zevulun were two of Leah's children. The two brothers made a pact. Yissachar would study Torah all day and Zevulun would go out into the world and conduct business. Zevulun would then return home and split his profits fifty-fifty with Yissachar. Reciprocally, half of the merits of Yissachar's Torah study would be transferred to Zevulun. In order for one to be able to engage in full-time Torah study, there must be those who support Torah learning. Thus the first *shin* in Yissachar—representing the active partner, Yissachar—is pronounced. But the second *shin*—representing the *silent* partner, Zevulun—remains mute.[8]

The above theme is underscored within the actual structure of the word Yissachar. Yissachar, יששכר, can be divided into two words: יש שכר,[9] *yesh s'char*, meaning "there is reward." This translation alludes directly to Zevulun and his sponsorship. It is also consistent with the last *mishnah* in Tractate *Uktzin*. The *mishnah* states: "In the future, G-d will bequeath to each *tzaddik* and *tzaddik* (i.e., each and every *tzaddik*) 310 worlds." What constitutes these 310 worlds? The Alter Rebbe explains in *Likkutei Torah*:[10] "As Jews we have 613 *mitzvos* and 7 Rabbinical laws which equal 620, the same as the *gematria* of *Kesser*, crown. As the *Sefirah* of *Kesser* represents the world of pleas-

---

8 Another two traditional reasons are found in the classical work *Daas Zekeinim m'Baalei Tosfos*, which comments on *Genesis* 30:14.

9 See *Or HaChaim* on *Numbers* 26:23. Also found in *B'nei Yissaschar* by R. Tzvi Elimelech of Dinov.

10 *Behaalos'cha*, p. 34a.

ure, it is thus the ultimate level of reward for doing *mitzvos*. The 310 worlds are exactly half."

One can say that the division of the 620 worlds reflects the division of rewards between the *tzaddik* Yissachar and the *tzaddik* Zevulun. This too is mirrored within the word יש שכר: *yesh* equals 310: י=10, ש=300. The 310 (*yesh*) worlds serve as a reward (*s'char*) for Zevulun for his partnership with Yissachar.

In the name of his father Rabbi Levi Yitzchak Schneerson,[11] the Rebbe explains that there are two levels to the Torah: the level that is revealed, the *Talmud* and *Halachah*, and the level that is concealed, *Kabbalah* and *Chassidus*. The revealed level is pronounced, thus the first *shin* of Yissachar. But the second *shin*, the concealed level, remains silent.

Gematria

The numerical value of *shin* is three hundred.[12] We know that the number one hundred represents perfection. In the academic world, scoring one hundred percent on an exam is considered impeccable. The same concept holds true in Judaism. If a person constitutes three unwavering lines of thought, speech, and action, then he is perfect. This person is thus represented by the number three hundred. All three of his columns are one hundred percent.

The *shin*, which stands for *shuvah* (penitence), also represents the Day of Atonement—Yom Kippur. The *gematria* of the word *kapper* ("atonement") is 300: *kaf* = 20, *pei* = 80 and *reish* = 200. The day of Yom Kippur is the power generator that gives a person the potential to be perfect throughout the entire year. When we atone (*kapper*=300) for our sins on Yom Kippur, we

---

11 *Sefer HaArachim Chabad, Osios,* letter *shin,* p. 453.
12 The number 300 represents beauty, נאה (*Mishnah Tamid* 2:2). *Sefer HaSichos 5750,* p. 669; see also *Shulchan Aruch of the Alter Rebbe,* vol. I, ch. 25:9.

have the potential to reach the perfection of the *shin*, which is 300.

Alternately, if the letter *shin* is spelled out, שין, its *gematria* is 360: *shin* = 300, *yud* = 10, *nun* = 50. There are 12 months in a year. The average month is 30 days.[13] 12 times 30 is 360. Thus the atonement of Yom Kippur (where *shin* = 360) has an effect on the entire year (which has an average of 360 days).[14]

Meaning

The letter *shin* has five definitions.[15] The first is *shein*, which means "tooth," or "teeth." The second is *lo shanisi*, meaning "steadfastness in one's faith." The third is *shinoy*, which is "to change for the good." The fourth is *shuvah*, which means "to return." The fifth is *shanah*, or "year."

The general use of one's teeth (*shein*) is to chew food. The teeth break up and grind food. This action represents an individual who carefully "chews over," or is careful with his actions. Additionally, the teeth represent strength. Many times, if we don't have the strength to break something with our hands, we use our teeth.

This strength brings us to the next interpretation of the *shin*, which is *lo shinisi*, he who does not change. This exemplifies the individual who is strong in his faith. He may move to another locale. The weather may wax hot or cold. The state of his work or finances may fluctuate. But this individual has the ability to remain strong and not be swayed by the circumstances of his life.

The *shin* also represents the concept of *shinoy*, which is to change for the good. When a person realizes that he has faults,

---

13 *Sefer HaArachim Chabad, loc. cit.,* pp. 452-453, fn. 365.

14 *Likkutei Levi Yitzchak,* Commentary on *Tanach,* p. 37. There he also explains that the word *hashanah,* which literally means "the year," has the *gematria* of 360. Also see *Sefer HaArachim Chabad, loc. cit.,* p. 453.

15 *Ibid.,* pp. 421-424.

that he is not perfect in his intellect, understanding and knowledge, or in his thought, speech and action, he makes an attempt
to improve these qualities.

This ability to change has a direct connection to the concept
of *shuvah*, which means to return—to return to the path of the
three Patriarchs: Abraham, Isaac and Jacob. As Jews, we've
inherited our forefathers' connection to G-d: the quality of love
from Abraham, awe from Isaac, and mercy from Jacob. Every
Jew can always return to G-d.

This leads us to the last interpretation of *shin*, *shanah*, which
means "year." A year contains four seasons. Fall is the time
when one enters the business world following a month full of
holidays: Rosh Hashanah, Yom Kippur and Sukkos. Winter is a
span of coldness and indifference. Spring embodies a period of
rebirth and growth. It reminds us not to be complacent, but
rather to constantly grow in G-dliness and humanity. And the
heat of summer arouses the body's passions. Throughout every
aspect of seasonal change, one must remain steadfast in one's
faith in G-d. The four seasons are echoed in the four lines of the
shin. The antidote for the challenges inherent in each of the
four seasons is the four Matriarchs. Their love and consistency
nurture our growth from one season to the next.

Rosh Hashanah is also connected to the letter *shin*. The *Mishnah* tells us that there are three different Rosh Hashanahs. This
is reflected in the *shin's* three different lines—each representing
one of the three *shanim*, or heads of the year. There's yet
another opinion positing that there are four heads to the year.[16]
This is signified by the *shin* with four lines or heads.

---

16 It states in tractate *Rosh Hashanah* 1:1 that the first of Nissan is the new year for kings and
holidays, and the first of Tishrei is the new year for calendar years, for the tithing of animals,
and for planting. The fifteenth of Shevat is the new year for trees. According to the *Tanna
Kamma*, the first of Elul is actually the new year for animal tithing, which would make it the
fourth new year.

According to Chassidic philosophy, there is actually another Rosh Hashanah. One can say that this is symbolized by the crown on the letter *shin*. This Rosh Hashanah occurs on the 19th of Kislev, the day the Alter Rebbe was released from prison in 1798. The Alter Rebbe had been incarcerated due ultimately to his authorship of the *Tanya*, known as the "written law" of *Chabad Chassidus*. Tragically, he was slandered by some of his fellow Jews, who felt that his mystical text was too radical for the prevailing current of Jewish thought. These adversaries reported the Alter Rebbe to the authorities, and he was subsequently arrested for treason.

The 19th of Kislev is not only celebrated by chassidim, it has been acknowledged by the leaders of the Lithuanian *yeshivah* world as well, including Rabbi Chaim "Brisker" Soloveitchik and Rabbi Chaim Ozer Grodzinsky of Vilna, as depicted in the opening stories of this chapter.

It should be noted that the 19th of Kislev is known to chassidim as "the holiday of holidays."[17] In Judaism, every holiday is referred to as a Festival of Joy (*simchah*). Since Chassidic philosophy teaches that every day and everything one does must be infused with joy, the Chassidic new year is hence the *quintessence* and source of this joy.

Now, one of the things that makes the *shin* unique among the letters is that it can be placed in different places within the body of a word without changing the meaning of that word itself. It may, however, affect that word's spiritual significance.[18]

The classic example of this is the Hebrew word for "sheep." It can be spelled כשב (*kesev*) or כבש (*keves*). A sheep was the traditional twice-daily sacrifice in the days of the First and Second Holy Temples. Both words contain the exact same three letters. In *kesev*, the *shin* comes before the *beis*. But in *keves*,

---

17 *Likkutei Sichos*, vol. 35, p. 279.
18 *Sefer HaArachim Chabad, loc. cit.*, p. 448.

the *beis* precedes the *shin*. We know that the letter *kaf* represents *Kesser*, the crown of G-d, representing G-d's will and pleasure. The *beis* is the human intellect, which is generally divided into two aspects: the concept and the actual apprehension of that idea. The letter *shin* represents the three columns of one's emotions (*Chessed, Gevurah, Tiferes*). Now, the sequence of human behavior typically follows the established pattern of *keves*: First comes a person's desire for pleasure *(kaf)*. The next step is the *beis*, intellect, bringing that desire into a cognitive design. This process finally leads to the emotions *(shin)* which lead to the goal's fulfillment.

Sometimes, however, one is able to bypass the intellect by employing the emotions to bring the desire to fruition. For example, the emotional stress of a deadline will give a person the strength to stay up all night and perform in a superhuman fashion. Were the intellect his sole motivator, the job would most likely be performed in a more methodical, but less efficient manner. That's the word *kesev*. Instead of the *beis* (intellect) directly following the *kaf* (*kesser*), we first have the *shin*, the three columns of emotions. The *beis*, intellect, comes last. When a person has this ability to positively employ his emotions before his intellect, he exemplifies the concept of *shtus de kedushah*—suprarational spiritual folly (as discussed in the chapter on the letter *kuf*).

This aspect of *kesev* is exemplified by the way the Jews held on to their Jewish traditions and customs during the seventy years of Communism in the former Soviet Union and Eastern Europe. They had every reason to give up their Jewish practice. According to Torah law, one isn't required to die for Judaism. One doesn't have to give up one's life to keep Shabbos. One doesn't have to die to fulfill the *mitzvah* of praying three times daily, or studying Torah. Yet throughout the course of history many Jews proclaimed with pride, "We will continue to live as Jews even if we have to die in the process."

Chanukah represents that same aspect. When the saga of Chanukah unfolded, it wasn't the Jews' physical bodies that were in danger, it was their spiritual lives. The Syrian-Greeks said, "Live in Israel. We will not harm you. Just follow *our* law. Don't circumcise your children. Don't keep Shabbos. Don't study the Torah." But the innermost spark within the Jewish people, their connection to G-d, surpassed their intellect. It was because of this that they were willing to sacrifice their lives— and ultimately were rewarded with victory over their enemies and the discovery of a single cruse of oil that lasted miraculously for eight complete days. Again, we see the operative nature of *kesev* when the emotions of the *shin* precede the intellect of the *beis*.

The sheep (*keves* or *kesev*), humble by nature, follows its master, the shepherd. It is completely subservient to G-d's will. As a result it is used as a sacrifice on the altar to be one with G-d. This is the letter *shin*, the letter that unites a person with G-d.

Tav

TAV—PERFECTION

Design	1. *Dalet* and *nun*
	2. three lines and a *yud*
Gematria	Four hundred
Meaning	1. Truth 2. sign 3. life or death

Once, when the Rebbe Rashab was four or five years old, he came crying to his grandfather the Tzemach Tzedek. The Tzemach Tzedek asked, "Dear child, why are you crying?"

The Rashab said, "I just learned in *cheder* that G-d revealed Himself to Abraham."

"So why are you crying?"

The Rashab answered, "G-d revealed Himself to Abraham, but why doesn't G-d reveal Himself to me?"

His grandfather explained that a man who is ninety-nine years old and willing to follow G-d's command to circumcise himself is worthy of G-d's revelation. Even after a man elevates himself ninety-nine levels, a level of near perfection, he must retain his humility before G-d.

Design

The twenty-second and final letter of the *alef-beis* is the letter *tav*.

The design of the *tav* is a *dalet* and a *nun*. These two letters spell out the name of Dan, דן, one of the tribes of Israel. In the desert, the twelve tribes of Israel were divided into four camps. When the tribes set out to travel, the camp of Dan was the last to proceed. If any of the other tribes left something behind, the tribe of Dan would collect and return it.

The *Talmud* states:[1] "Who is called a fool? One who loses what (*mah*) has been given to him." On a deeper level, the concept of "what has been given to him," represented by the Hebrew word *mah*, denotes the state of humility. One who is humble says, "*Mah*—What [am I]? I am nothing before G-d."

A Jew, whose soul has its source in G-d Himself, is naturally humble. By losing this humility, that which "has been given to him," that individual throws away his connection to his soul, and is considered a fool. The tribe of Dan thus had the ability to

1 *Chagigah* 4a.

return the holiness and humility (the *mah*) to the other tribes of Israel.[2]

The importance of Dan can be seen by way of analogy to the human body. A body has a head, hands, and feet. At first glance, the head is greater than the feet due to its intellectual superiority. But a head cannot reach its destination unless it is transported there by the feet. The tribe of Dan comprises the feet of the Jewish people. It represents the level of bringing the head to its destination. How? Through humility. The head is, quite literally, the brains of the operation. This often results in arrogance, as when something "goes to your head." The feet, on the other hand, have no brains. They work all day long transporting us to our destinations but never get any recognition or honor. Reflecting on the humble service of the feet can bring us to humility.

The heel of the foot has no feeling or knowledge. Placing the heel of one's foot inside a shoe, where it's dark, represents the concept of accepting the yoke of Heaven in a cold, dark world. Just as the feet are the foundation and the support of the human body, so, too, accepting the yoke of G-d is the foundation of Judaism. One must have the humility to accept the will of G-d beyond question and beyond rational understanding. It is the letter *tav*, the letter of humility, that allows the individual to ongoingly embrace the love of G-d and Torah which all too easily can be left behind through human ego and arrogance.

On a practical level, the word *dan* means "to judge." A Jew realizes that he must judge his every action before performing it. By looking into the *Shulchan Aruch, the Code of Jewish Law,* the Jew learns that the performance of every action, whether actual law or beyond the letter of the law, has its own circumscribed areas, responsibilities, and particulars. By acknowledg-

2 *Likkutei Sichos,* vol. 1, pp. 103-104.

ing the authority of the *Code of Jewish Law*, one is able to fulfill all of G-d's laws to the fullest degree. Again, this only comes through humility. If a person were to rely only on his mind and intellect, he might succumb to arrogance and convince himself that one commandment or another is not really that important. For the "important" commandments—like Shabbos or idolatry—he'll follow the law to the letter. But as for the "little" ones—like where to place the *mezuzah*, putting on *tefillin* daily, or the particulars about keeping kosher—he does not have to be so scrupulous. It does not really matter to him what the *Shulchan Aruch* says. The tribe of Dan comes to teach that true submission to G-d's laws, with all their aspects and ramifications, requires self-judgment and humility.

Another aspect of the *dalet* and *nun* of the *tav* relates to the separate characteristics of each letter. As explained earlier in the chapter on *dalet*, *dalet* can mean both poverty (*dal*) and being raised up (*dilisoni*). The interpretation the *dalet* assumes is the result of the specific aspect of its companion *nun*.

As stated previously, the letter *nun* represents *ona'ah*, deceit. There are two types of deceit. There is *ona'ah* which ultimately ends in pain and destruction, as it states:[3] "And he repays His enemies [in their lifetime] to make them perish." Although in this case the recipient is completely absorbed by the pursuit of self-indulgent pleasure, he is actually being deceived, because in the long run he will suffer.

Then there is *ona'ah* that results in a person being rewarded and uplifted. When G-d created the world, He concealed Himself within the laws of nature: the "ultimate deception." When one toils to find the truth buried within the deception and restricts oneself to the laws of Torah to do so, although this route may be temporarily difficult, one will ultimately find G-d and forever bask in the pleasures of Paradise.

3 *Deuteronomy* 7:10.

When the *nun* is the former, the *dalet* becomes that of poverty. If one engages in excessive or lustful pleasure, he will
eventually come to sin. He will not take the time to connect to
G-d and appreciate the spiritual blessings in his life because he
will always be craving and running after more pleasure. So
although this indulgent pleasure may initially seem glorious, it
eventually leads to poverty.[4]

When the *nun* represents the latter, leading to progressive
revelations of G-dliness and self-refinement, then the *dalet* is
exalted and the individual is uplifted.

Pertaining to the generation of the Flood, the Torah tells us
that Noah was a *tzaddik* "in his generation" (*b'dorosov*). The
word בדרתיו, *b'dorosov*, can be broken up into two words: *b'doro*
and *tav*.[5] The sin of Noah's generation was thus the letter *tav*,
an excess of pleasure, as reflected in its "excessive" *nun*. G-d
allowed the people of that time to do whatever they wanted. He
did not restrict them or punish them for their wrongdoings.
Rather, G-d let them go on and on until they were so lost it was
impossible for them to return to Him. The only way G-d could
rectify the world at that point was by destroying it through the
Flood.

The Rebbe explains another element of the *tav's* design.[6] The
tav is made up of three lines. In this sense it is similar to the
hei, which also has three lines: two vertical and one horizontal.
They represent Torah study (thought), prayer (speech), and the
performance of good deeds (action). Because it is the last letter
and thus the culmination of the *alef-beis*, the *tav* represents
someone who is perfect on all these levels. However, the condition of being "perfect" can also result in arrogance. Therefore,
the *yud* in the lower left-hand corner completes the *tav* to lend

4 *Sefer HaArachim Chabad, Osios,* letter *tav,* p. 472ff.
5 For grammatical reasons, the *tav* is pronounced as a *sav* in this case.
6 *Sefer HaSichos 5751,* vol. 2, p. 665.

it humility. When a person knows he is perfect and that he has ended his service by fulfilling his level or destiny, he must arrive at the *yud* of humility. We see this in the design of the *tav*.

When Abraham was ninety-nine years old and essentially perfect, G-d told him to circumcise himself. G-d said, If you will circumcise yourself (also symbolic of the removal of the ego),[7] *then* you will be "perfect." Why? Because if one is perfect in his own eyes without the aspect of humility, there is no true perfection. One can only be perfect when one circumcises his ego.

Gematria

The numerical value of *tav* is four hundred. We find the number four hundred mentioned frequently in the Torah. One instance is when Abraham needed to buy a burial place for his wife, Sarah.[8] The Torah tells us that he went to Ephron, the leader of the Hittite people, in the city of Hebron and asked him for a piece of land. Ephron responded that he would sell the parcel for four hundred shekels. The name Ephron, עפרן, has the *gematria* of 400: *ayin* = 70, *pei* = 80, *reish* = 200, and *nun* = 50. Significantly, Hebron was the first city in the land of Israel to be officially purchased by the Jewish people.[9]

---

7 *Deuteronomy* 30:6.

8 *Genesis* 23:4, 15.

9 It is for this reason that the Jewish people are entirely justified in claiming ownership of Hebron, and particularly the Cave of Machpelah. We bought it; it belongs to us.

It is relevant here to cite the *Code of Jewish Law* (*Shabbos*, ch. 329:6), which states:

"When there is a [Jewish] city close to the border, then even if [enemies mount an attack, although they] come only for the purpose of [taking] straw and stubble, we should [take up arms] and desecrate the Sabbath because of them. For [if we do not prevent their coming,] they may conquer the city, and from there the [rest of the] land will be easy for them to conquer."

A Jew has the obligation to lift up arms against this band, even on Shabbos, even if the enemy does not pose an immediate danger to life. This law has no greater relevance than in contemporary Israel. A border city like Hebron is the key to an entire country. By surrendering it to another nation and diminishing the land of Israel, one puts all of Israel's

Furthermore, the letter *tav* in the "small *gematria*," is four.[10]
The cave where Sarah was buried is called the "cave of the four
couples," as Adam and Chava (Eve), Abraham and Sarah, Isaac
and Rebecca, and Jacob and Leah are all buried there.

Four hundred also represents the four hundred worlds of
pleasure that the righteous people will acquire in the World to
Come.[11] The Land of Israel, according to the dimensions in the
Torah, measures 400 by 400 *mil* (a *mil* is approximately 1
kilometer).

The number four hundred is also found pertaining to the
"Covenant between the Parts,"[12] when G-d caused Abraham to
fall into a deep slumber and told him that his children would
reside in a foreign land (the land of Egypt) for four hundred
years and afterwards go out with great wealth and an out-
stretched arm.

Yet another instance of four hundred is found in the account
of Jacob's encounter with his brother Esau after sojourning
twenty years in the house of Laban. When Jacob approaches
Esau he is informed that Esau is mighty, for he has with him
four hundred men. As a result, Jacob sends forth a messenger to
tell Esau, "I sojourned (*garti*) in Laban's house for twenty
years."[13] The word *garti*, גרתי, ("sojourned") has the *gematria* of
613, and is synonymous with the 613 commandments. What
Jacob thus communicated to his brother was, "Though I lived in
the house of this wicked Laban, I did not violate any of the 613

citizens in grave danger. There are those today who propose that giving land to the Arabs
will facilitate the peace process. But the *Shulchan Aruch*, which is the very measure of our
halachah and tradition, states that such a transfer will only end in peril. Every *inch* of Israel
is in fact a border city.

10 For an explanation of "the small *gematria*," *mispar katan*, see chapter on the letter *zayin*.

11 Or *HaTorah*, p. 1895, explains the 400 worlds of pleasure spoken of in the *Zohar* to be the
same as the 310 worlds mentioned in the *Mishnah* (see end of "Design" section in the
chapter on the letter *shin*). However, the *Zohar* considers the "10" or *yud* of 310 to be
complete, i.e., 10x10=100. It therefore totals 400.

12 *Genesis* 15:9-13.

13 *Ibid.* 32:5.

commandments." The word *garti* can also mean to live as a foreigner.[14] When it came to Jacob's physical existence, the materialistic aspects of life, he lived as a foreigner, meaning that he recognized materialism and physicality as merely the means to serve G-d, not as an end in themselves. This gave him the strength to keep the whole Torah. Twenty times twenty[15] equals four hundred. Therefore after his twenty years of refinement, Jacob now possessed the ability to overcome the four hundred men of Esau.

Finally, the numerical value of *tav* can represent both the four hundred levels of evil and the four hundred sparks of G-dliness that are found in the world. The *tav* thus embodies the ability to transform these negative energies into positive sparks.

Meaning

It states in the *Talmud*[16] that the letter *tav* represents the word אמת, *emes*, meaning truth. The reason *emes* is represented by its last letter (*tav*) and not its first (*alef*) is that the essence of truth is determined at the end of a journey or passage, not at the beginning. Often when we begin something, the truth of the matter does not seem attractive. Only upon seeing the outcome do we appreciate that the path of *emes* was the only way to travel.

This is the reason for using the *tav* to signify אמת. If the Sages of the *Talmud* needed a letter to symbolize truth, why didn't they pick the א, the first letter of *emes*? Because the letter *tav* represents humankind's ultimate destination, the culmination of our Divine service to perfect the world. And this truth will be unveiled in the final stages of the coming of *Mashiach*.

---

14 *Likkutei Sichos,* vol. 1, p. 68.
15 Signifying the dual dimensions of positive and negative, light and dark, that exist in everything.
16 *Shabbos* 104a.

Additionally, the *Talmud* comments that the word *sheker*, or falsehood (the antithesis of *emes*), is written with the letters *shin*, *kuf* and *reish*: the last three letters in the *alef-beis* before the *tav*. *Emes*, meanwhile, is spelled *alef*, *mem* and *tav*: the first, middle, and last letter of the *alef-beis*. The question is, why are the letters of *emes* so spread out in contrast to those of *sheker*? The *Talmud* concludes that the letters of *sheker* are close to-gether because falsehood is very common. Truth, on the other hand, is very hard to find. This is depicted by the vast expanse between its letters.

In Psalm 119 it states:[17] "Your very first utterance is truth." There are several commentaries regarding this passage. One states that the first letter of the Ten Commandments is an *alef* (*Anochi*). The first letter of the *Mishnah* is a *mem* (*M'eimasai*). The first letter of the *Gemara* is a *tav* (*Tanna*). *Alef*, *mem* and *tav* spell the word *emes*.

Furthermore, the *Talmud* states: "The signature of G-d is the word *emes*."[18] Just as every artist puts his signature on his paintings, G-d imbeds His signature in the universe, His crea-tion. This concept is found in the *Zohar* in its explanation of the last three words in the story of Creation: "...*bara Elokim laasos*[19]—[He rested from all His work] which G-d created and made." The final letters of these three words, ברא אלקים לעשות, spells the word *emes*. Why? Because G-d's painting is imbued with His signature of truth.

On Shabbos, the purpose of G-d's creation becomes clear. G-d formed the world for humankind to rectify—*laasos*. By fulfilling Torah and *mitzvos* and increasing our acts of goodness and kindness, we make the world a better place in which to live. In such a fashion we bring G-d—*truth*—into the world.

17 V. 160.
18 *Shabbos* 55a.
19 *Genesis* 2:3.

Finally, the *Tanya*[20] tells us that G-d is called *emes* because the only real truth is G-d.

The Rebbe explains that the word *emes* is comprised of an *alef* and the word *mes*. *Alef* represents G-d, the Creator of the universe. If one removes the *alef* from the word *emes*, he is left with *mes*, which means "death."

The actual meaning of *tav* is "sign." In *Ezekiel*[21] it states that when G-d was about to destroy the Holy Temple he told His angel to put a mark on the foreheads of the people. That mark was the letter *tav*. Those who were righteous received the letter in ink. Those who were wicked received the letter in blood.

The *tav* can represent *ticheyeh*, which means "life." But it can also represent the word *tamus*, which means "death." *Tav's* meaning as "sign" thus remains consistent with the dichotomous nature of its *gematria*, four hundred, having both a positive and negative aspect (i.e., the four hundred spiritual worlds of pleasure vs. the four hundred men of Esau). And because the *tav* is the last letter of the *alef-beis*, this duality takes on a special importance. The *tav*, coming at the end of the twenty-two letters of the *alef-beis* with all of their ramifications and meanings on both the revealed and esoteric levels—could all too easily become overconfident: "I finished the entire set of letters. I accomplished what every letter stands for. Look how perfect I am."

The message of the *tav*, however, is an eternal lesson for us. It tells us that if we continue to pursue the instruction of the Torah with humility, then this is *ticheyeh*, life. If, however, we seek this truth through arrogance, it is *tamus*; the antithesis of true living.

As stated above, the left leg of the letter *tav* incorporates the *yud*. Once we have absorbed each of the letters of the *alef-beis*

20 *Iggeres HaKodesh*, Epistle 6.
21 9:4.

representing the entire Torah, we must not forget that the ultimate level, the foundation of the entire *alef-beis*, is the *yud* of humility.

By embracing this humility, one is empowered to live the precepts of the Torah with a pure soul and a joyful heart. The performance of these commandments will reveal the essential quality of the twenty-two letters of light—the ultimate state that will accompany the imminent days of *Mashiach*.

נקודות

The Nekudos—Vowels

Nekudos Chart[1]
PRONUNCIATION AND GEMATRIA

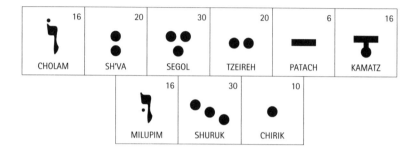

1 *Siddur Tehillat Hashem.* There are three additional vowel variations on the chart there that will not be addressed in this chapter.

INTRODUCTION

For six months, Joab, King David's fierce general, warred against and killed all the males of the evil nation of Amalek.[1]

When he finally returned, he told the king of his great victory and how he had slain all the men of Amalek, to which King David responded, "The Torah commands us to destroy the *entire* nation of Amalek, including the women and the children.[2] Why did you kill only the men?"

Joab answered that the Torah explicitly states:[3] "...*timcheh et zachar* (זָכָר) *Amalek*—you shall destroy the males (*zachar*) of Amalek."

King David replied, "You have read the word with the wrong vowels (*nekudos*). It is not זָכָר, *zachar*, but זֵכֶר, *zeicher*, which means the 'remembrance' [of every member of Amalek]."

Joab then went to his childhood teacher and rebuked him for mispronouncing the word *zeicher* as *zachar*. His teacher replied, "On the contrary, I taught you correctly with the word *zeicher*, remembrance, implying our obligation to destroy the entire nation of Amalek. I'm sorry, but the mistake was yours, Joab."

How could Joab have made such a mistake?

Like the letters, the *nekudos*, or vowels, are also of Divine origin. Given by G-d to Moses on Mount Sinai, they were

---

1 *Bava Basra* 21a,b; *I Kings* 11:15-16.
2 *Rashi* on *Deuteronomy* 25:19.
3 *Deuteronomy, ibid.*

passed down orally[4] from leader to leader until they reached
Ezra the Scribe,[5] who revealed and taught them to the Jewish
nation. Up until that point, Hebrew was never written with
vowels and the commoner didn't even know they existed. The
incident with Joab took place approximately 500 years before
Ezra revealed the vowels—hence the justification for his error.

In *Sefer Pardes*[6] and *Tikkunei Zohar*[7] it's explained that each
vowel is representative of one of the ten *Sefiros*, and that each
one has a *gematria* and a meaning. The names of the vowels are
not only holy, they also carry the initials and acronyms of
angels.

The writings on Hebrew grammar explain that if the letter is
the "body," then the vowel is its soul. A body without a soul
cannot survive. One can thus begin to appreciate both the
spiritual energy transmitted via the *nekudos* and what they
represent.

The vowels, like the letters, can also be explained on the three
levels of design, *gematria*, and meaning. The *gematria* can be
computed on several levels. The simplest level is that each dot,
similar to the *yud*, equals ten, and each line (horizontal or
vertical; similar to that of the *vav*) represents six.

---

4 *Or HaTefillah*, vol. 1, p. 5, compiled by Rabbi Y. Alperowitz, Kehot Publication Society,
   Brooklyn, NY, 1989.
5 5th century BCE.
6 *Shaar HaNekudos.*
7 *Or HaTefillah*, vol. 1, p. 6.

KAMATZ—CONCEALMENT

Design and Sefirah

The *kamatz* is designed as a straight line, similar to a horizontal *vav*. It has a dot beneath it, similar to the *yud*. The *kamatz* represents *Kesser*,[8] the crown, and is the first and the highest of the *Sefiros*.

Gematria

The *gematria* of the *kamatz* comprises six (the straight line) and ten (the dot) for a total of sixteen.

Meaning

The word *kamatz* means to "close and conceal." In the Holy Temple, the *Kohen* would take the meal offerings and close his fingers around the flour (as it states in the Torah, "*vekamatz*"[9]), concealing it in his hand.

When one pronounces the sound of the *kamatz*, "aw," one actually closes one's lips.[10] To form the sound of the *patach*, "ah," one does the opposite. The *patach*, which means "to open," is formed by opening the lips.

Kamatz is an acronym for "צח אור מצוחצח אור קדמון אור‎—The primordial, bright, and pure light." This level of illumination is so overwhelming that one cannot fully appreciate or internalize it. Rather one can only have a glimpse—like looking into a

8 *Or HaTefillah*, vol. 1, p. 14.
9 *Leviticus* 2:2.
10 *Tanya, Iggeres HaKodesh*, Epistle 5.

mirror and seeing the form of an object but not the essence of
the object.[11] This primordial energy is "*kamatz*," concealed from
the average person.

As an interesting note, the word *Mashiach* begins with a
kamatz beneath the letter *mem*. *Mashiach* will reveal the
concealed levels of Torah and Creation.

11 *Or HaTorah, Bamidbar,* p. 1,492.

■

PATACH—TO OPEN

Design and Sefirah

The *patach* is displayed as a straight line (similar to a horizontal *vav*). The *patach* represents the *Sefirah* of *Chochmah*[12]—the flash of an idea or wisdom. It alludes to the horizontal line of thought, as explained in the letter *hei*.

Gematria

The numerical value of the *patach* is six, corresponding to the *gematria* of the letter *vav*.

Meaning

To open; to have a glimmer of what was previously closed and to acquire knowledge.

---

12 *Or HaTefillah*, vol. 1, p. 11.

TZEIREH—UNDERSTANDING

Design and Sefirah

The *tzeireh* is configured as two dots side by side. They represent the *Sefirah* of *Binah*—understanding. *Pardes Rimonim*[13] explains that the two dots signify the two luminaries, the sun and the moon, as well as the *tzaddik* and the *baal teshuvah*. When the Jewish people do *teshuvah* and *Mashiach* comes, G-d will restore the moon to its original glory, commensurate with the power of the sun.

The teachings of *Chassidus* additionally explain that the two dots represent *ratzo* and *shov;*[14] the passion of prayer that runs to expire into G-d's light, and the returning calmness of Torah study, also referred to as fire and water.

In addition, *ratzo* and *shov* are also interpreted as the self-nullification one experiences from spiritual bliss to the point of expiry, followed by a return to the material world to fulfill one's mission in a body.

Gematria

The numerical value of the *tzeireh* is twenty (ten for each dot, or *yud*). During the time when the Holy Temple stood, the weight of one shekel, one coin, was twenty *gerah*. Each Jew was commanded to give a half-shekel annually to be used for the daily communal sacrifices. Only when two Jews gave a half-

13 *Shaar HaNekudos.* Ch. 4.
14 *Or HaTefillah*, p. 15.

shekel each, did they have a complete shekel of twenty, representing Jewish unity. The Rebbe explains that this exemplifies one's ability to be complete only when one bonds with another.

Tzeireh, which is twenty, can be broken down into ten and ten,[15] representing the Ten Utterances of Creation which are dependent upon the Ten Commandments.[16]

Meaning

The *Tikkunei Zohar* states[17] that the *tzeireh* means *vayitzer* (*Genesis* 2:7), "to form." This definition is consistent with *Binah*, the level of understanding that forms and elaborates on *Chochmah*, the flash of an idea.

Furthermore, it states in the *Zohar* and the *Tikkunim*[18] that *Binah* represents the higher of the two levels of *teshuvah*. It is through this higher level of repentance that the moon is restored to its original strength, after *Mashiach's* arrival.

One can draw a parallel between the word *tzeireh* (representing *teshuvah*) and *tzari* (balm or remedy), which share the same letters. As it states:[19] "Is there no balm (*tzari*) in Gilead?" And the *Talmud*[20] tells us, "Great is *teshuvah* for it brings remedy to the world."

15 *Zohar III*, 11b.
16 This concept is also mentioned in the chapter on the letter *vav* and *kaf.*
17 P. 7b.
18 *Tanya, Iggeres HaKodesh*, ch. 9.
19 *Jeremiah* 8:22.
20 *Yoma* 86a.

SEGOL—THE PATRIARCHS

Design and Sefirah
The *segol* represents the *Sefirah* of *Chessed*[21]—kindness—and is displayed as a triangle of three dots: right, left and center.

Gematria
The numerical value of the *segol* is thirty.

Meaning
The Jewish people are called "*am segulah*,"[22] a chosen people. Just as the *segol* is made up of three points, the people of Israel are composed of *Kohanim*, Levites, and Israelites.

The *segol* also represents the Patriarchs: Abraham, Isaac and Jacob. Alternatively, the *segol* signifies the three founding fathers of *Chassidus*.

The first, the Baal Shem Tov, is mirrored in the right dot. The right dot introduces the three loves: love of G-d, love of Torah, and love for a fellow Jew.

The left dot signifies the Maggid of Mezritch, the successor to the Baal Shem Tov, who taught only those who were great Torah scholars and men of extreme piety.

The middle dot, representing Rabbi Schneur Zalman of Liadi (the Alter Rebbe), incorporates the teachings of both the Baal Shem Tov and the Maggid. The Alter Rebbe perpetuated and

---

21 *Or HaTefillah*, vol. 1, p. 8.
22 *Deuteronomy* 7:6.

augmented their efforts by making the esoteric teachings of *Chassidus* accessible to all people.

SH'VA—FIRST VOWEL OF CREATION

Design and Sefirah

The *sh'va* is displayed as two dots, one on top of the other. The *sh'va* embodies the spiritual aspect of *Gevurah*[23]—judgment and discipline. According to the *Tikkunei Zohar*,[24] the *sh'va* represents G-d's use of *Gevurah* in minimizing the moon and making it smaller than the sun.

Additionally, the positioning of one dot atop the other declares the higher point's domination and greatness.

Gematria

The numerical value of the *sh'va* is twenty.

Meaning

According to *Kabbalah*,[25] the *sh'va* is spelled *shin, beis, alef—*שבא*—*and not *shin, vav, alef—*שוא*. Sh'va* with a *vav* connotes vanity and falsehood because the word *shav*, falsehood, is spelled *shin, vav, alef. Sh'va* with a *beis*, however, means "to sit"—ישב.

The function of the *sh'va* is to separate a word into syllables and "slow down" the word's pronunciation, as in the word בְּרֵאשִׁית—or *be-rei-shis*. The *sh'va* under the *beis* separates the first syllable of the word from the latter two. The *sh'va's* func-

---

23 *Or HaTefillah*, vol. 1, p. 8.
24 P. 7b.
25 *Ibid.*

tion is thus similar to the hyphen found in phonetic spellings in a dictionary.

The word *sh'va* gets its meaning "to sit" because it shares the same root letters with the word *yosheiv*, which means "sit" (or "dwell"). Therefore, when the *sh'va* is under a letter, it causes the letter to "sit" (or pause).

Indeed, the entire purpose of Creation was that G-d should "sit," so to speak – that is, to have "a dwelling place in this world."[26] Similarly, there is a Chassidic teaching which states:[27] "[Since] You [G-d] are Holy and elevated above the world, what causes You to 'sit' and become involved in worldly matters is that Your people praise You."

One can say then that the reason why the *sh'va* is the very first vowel of the Torah is that it hints to the purpose of Creation.

Additionally, *Kabbalah* explains[28] that G-d created the world with the attribute of *Gevurah* in order to condense and contract His infinite light. Perhaps this is another reason why the first *vowel* of the Torah is a *sh'va*, as it represents *Gevurah*. Just as we attribute significance to the *beis*, the first letter of the Torah, so, too, one can attribute importance to the first vowel of the Torah, the *sh'va*.

---

26 *Tanchuma, Nasso* 16. See also *Likkutei Sichos*, vol. 6, p.17.
27 *Likkutei Sichos*, vol. 7, p. 136ff., based on a verse in the Book of *Psalms* (22:4): "*V'Atah Kadosh, yosheiv tehillos Yisroel* – And You are Holy (set apart), *yosheiv* ('enthroned' from the root word 'to sit') due to the praises of Your people Israel."
28 *Tanya, Shaar HaYichud VehaEmunah*, ch. 6.

CHOLAM—POWER TO FORGIVE

Design and Sefirah

The *cholam* is a dot that rests above a letter.[29] It refers to the *Sefirah* of *Tiferes*[30]—beauty or mercy. In general, a dot represents *Malchus*, the last of the ten *Sefiros*. *Malchus* (which literally means kingship) in fact represents "*bittul*" or self-nullification—considering oneself as a mere dot or speck on the face of the earth. Through the act of self-nullification, the dot is elevated to the degree of *Tiferes*.

Gematria

The numerical equivalent of the *cholam* is either ten or sixteen (depending upon whether it's a single dot on top of a letter, or atop a *vav*).

Meaning

Cholam means "strength."[31] In addition, when transposed, the letters of *cholam*, חלם, make up the words מלח, *melach* (salt), and מחל *machal* (forgiveness).[32] Salt was used as a preservative

---

29 When the dot is atop a *vav*, the vowel is comprised of both the *vav* and the dot.
30 *Likkutei Torah, Vayikra*, p. 6c.
31 See *Rashi* on Job 39:4.
32 *Likkutei Torah, loc. cit.*

and placed on every sacrifice in the Holy Temple to demonstrate that the merit of the sacrifice in procuring forgiveness for the sin remains forever, as it states:[33] "ברית מלח—an everlasting covenant of salt." The strength of salt is that it withstands the changes of time. Furthermore, when a person personifies strength, he has the perpetual power to forgive.

---

33 *Numbers* 18:19.

●

CHIRIK—FROZEN GIVER

Design and Sefirah
The *chirik* is a single dot beneath a letter and refers to the *Sefirah* of *Netzach*[34]—victory.

Gematria
The *chirik* has a numerical value of ten.

Meaning
The letters of *chirik*, חרק, read backwards, spell *kerach*, קרח,[35] which means "ice." The nature of water is to flow. Water also symbolizes the benefactor giving to the beneficiary. When water becomes frozen, however, it cannot flow, or give. A giver may often become great in his own eyes. This egotism freezes him, impeding his spiritual ascent. Yet the fact that he has become stuck assists him in realizing that he's not truly in charge; rather G-d is the primordial Mover. The egotist is thus nullified before G-d.

This manner of nullification is alluded to in the description of the Chariot of Ezekiel, as it states:[36] "It resembled awesome ice spread out over their heads." *Chassidus* tells us that this ice represents one's nullification before G-d.

---

34 *Likkutei Torah, Devarim*, p. 87b.
35 *Or HaTefillah*, vol. 1, p. 17.
36 1:22.

One who reaches this level of service to G-d has been victorious over his animal soul, representative of the *Sefirah* of *Netzach.*

SHURUK AND MILUPIM—BE FRUITFUL AND MULTIPLY

Design and Sefirah

Although these two *nekudos* differ graphically, they both make the sound of "oo." The *shuruk* is represented as three dots on a diagonal line placed underneath a letter; the *milupim* is formed from the letter *vav* with a dot in the middle of its left side. The *Sefirah* of the *shuruk* is *Hod*—acknowledgment. The *Sefirah* of the *milupim* is *Yesod*—reproduction.

Gematria

The numerical value of the *shuruk* is thirty. The *milupim* has a numerical equivalent of sixteen.

Meaning

The definition of the word *shuruk*[37] is a soft vine (*sareikah*) that produces only a few grapes and a small amount of wine.[38] Just as these grapes have not yet been fully formed and have not produced a large quantity of wine, this represents a person who is weak in his spiritual service.

---

37 *Isaiah* 5:2 and *Jeremiah* 2:21. Also see *Genesis* 49:11.
38 *Torah Or*, p. 47a.

The three dots of the *shuruk*[39] are very different from the three of the *segol*. The *segol* relates to the three Patriarchs, who were very close to G-d. The *shuruk*, meanwhile, represents one who is far from G-d (because the three dots are moving away from the letter). However, because this person also possesses the quality of *Hod* (i.e., he acknowledges that he's far from G-d), when he recognizes how awesome and loving G-d truly is, he changes course and approaches the letter, proceeding in the positive direction.

The word *milupim*, מלאופם, derives perhaps from the word "to fill," *mil'u*, מלאו, as in the verse:[40] "Be fruitful and multiply, and *fill* the land and conquer it."

The message of the *milupim* is to be fruitful and fill the land with children, students, and good deeds—not to be complacent but to strive always to accomplish more and more. This alludes to the Kabbalistic representation of *milupim*, which is the *Sefirah* of *Yesod*, the attribute of reproduction.

---

39 These dots represent loose grapes on a spindly cluster as opposed to the full, robust cluster of the dots of the *segol*. Thus its connection to the *word shuruk*, as described above.
40 *Genesis* 1:28.

AFTERWORD

The Rebbe comments[1] that the single dot's placement in three different positions to form three different vowels—*chirik*, beneath the letter; *milupim*, in the middle; and finally *cholam*, on the top—reflects three different levels in a person's service to G-d. While it's true that the letters of the *alef-beis* (in a Torah scroll) are preordained by G-d, it is up to us as individuals where we position the dot.

Though much has been predetermined in Heaven, it is in our power to wallow at the bottom level, to live a life of mediocrity in the middle, or to ascend, rising all the way to the top of our potential and our relationship with G-d. We have the free choice to decide how to live our life and what to make of it.

1 *Or HaTefillah*, vol. 1, p. 17.

Appendix 1

A Letter from the Sixth Lubavitcher Rebbe,
Rabbi Yosef Y. Schneersohn,[1]
On the Importance of Pronouncing Prayers Properly
(*Igros Kodesh*, Vol. 7, p. 142)

Writes the sixth Lubavitcher Rebbe: "I would like to appro-priate an amazing story which was printed in the Mattei Yehudah, by Rabbi Leib Oppenheim (published 1699-1700, with approbations by the Rabbis of Prague and Frankfort)"

I, [i.e., Rabbi Leib Oppenheim,] have seen a manuscript of the great Torah scholar, Rabbi Meir, Chief Rabbi and head of the Yeshivah of the Jewish community of Lvov. He found a story in the work of a certain Kabbalist, who copied from the manu-script of his Torah teacher, the great scholar Rabbi Mordechai Yoffe [c. 1535-1612, known as the *Levush*, after the title of his renowned works], of blessed memory:

There was a certain man by the name of Rabbi Azaria, son of Rabbi Yedidia, who was very saintly and a great ascetic, out-standing in his knowledge of *PaRDeS* [acronym for *Pshat, Remez, Drush, Sod*—levels of Scriptural interpretation embracing the full spectrum of Torah subjects from legal to mystical].

He appeared in a dream to his friend, Rabbi Gedalia, and told him, a year after his passing, that he had been brought before the Heavenly Court. They had told him: "Look up and see!"

"I saw what appeared to be small flowers, as many as the stars of the heavens. Immediately, a great fear fell upon me, and

---

all my limbs and my knees were trembling. I asked: 'What are these?'

"They answered me:

" 'These are the *nekudos* [Hebrew vowels] that you have mis-treated. In your prayers, you pronounced a *tzeireh* instead of a *sh'va*, and a *chirik* instead of a *shuruk*, and other substitutions. You also skipped over letters by not pausing between adjacent ones. Not one of these letters and *nekudos* that you have ever spoiled is missing from here. All of them are bringing accusations against you and demanding judgment, saying that this person has mistreated us and put us to shame, preventing us from becoming part of the Divine Crown.

" 'However, G-d loves justice. Your judgment has been decided that you will be reincarnated so that perhaps you will be able to correct the misdeed. If not for your good deeds that have protected you, your judgment would have been much more severe.' "

Appendix 2

Reshimos No. 169
From the Personal Notes of The Lubavitcher Rebbe,
Rabbi Menachem M. Schneerson:
"The Letter Vav Is the Letter of Emes [Truth]"
(*Zohar* III, 2a)

[The letter] *vav* [has the numerical value of six]. It refers to *Z'eir Anpin* [lit. "small faces"—the six lower Divine attributes in the exalted spiritual world of *Atzilus*, the main attribute being *Tiferes*, in the middle between the extremes of right and left], which is [therefore] called *emes* [the path of *truth*].

Vav [6], when counted together with its previous numbers, [the numerical value of the letters] *alef, beis, gimmel, dalet, hei* [1-2-3-4-5], totals 21, and 21 squared [21 x 21 = 441] is [the numerical value of the word] *emes* (Ramaz, [commentary of Rabbi Moshe Zacuto on the *Zohar*] *ibid.*).

Vav [6] ends in the same digit even when it is multiplied by itself any number of times. 6x6 = 36, 6 x 36 = 216, 6 x 216 = 1296, and so on. The total always ends with 6.

[Six] is integrally equal to its parts ([i.e.,] half of it (3), together with a third (2), and a sixth (1), total 6)—[as explained in the commentary of] Rabbi Abraham Ibn Ezra (*Exodus* 3:15). (Also 28—and other numbers—have the same quality, [i.e., half of it, 14, together with a quarter, 7, a seventh, 4, a fourteenth, 2, and a twenty-eighth, 1, add up to 28]).

Everything physical has six directions [equivalent to the end points of its three dimensions, height, length and width]. For a dot, line and surface [which lack all six directions] are only pictures [but not reality].

Vav [which in Hebrew serves as a prefix denoting "and"] combines opposites (as in the *vav* of *v'haNora* ["*and* the Awesome One" in the first blessing of the *Shemoneh Esreh* prayer, which distinguishes it from the previous attribute]).

When you begin a word with *vav* ["and"] it adds to the previous subject, and [also] separates from the previous subject.

Vav [as a prefix to a past or future verb in Scriptural Hebrew] converts from past to future tense and vice versa [future to past].

Vav [when spelled out phonetically—*vav, alef, vav*] has the same numerical value [13] as אחד, *echad* ["one"], for it [has the function of] combining and unifying.

Six [times the radius of a circle] equals [the circumference] of the circle [or three times its diameter, as we find in the *Talmud*:] "Whatever has a circumference of three hand-breadths has a width [diameter] of one hand-breadth" (*Eruvin* 13b).

Look up the introduction to *Tzemach David*[1] [where some of the above-mentioned properties of "Six" are explained].

---

1 A historic chronology by Rabbi David Ganz (1541-1613), a Torah scholar and expert mathematician and astronomer, who also authored a work on those subjects entitled *Nechmad Vena'im*. In his introduction to *Tzemach David*, he writes:

"The number 6 is a number that remains integral [even] in its parts, for a sixth is 1, a third is 2, and a half is 3, and when you add these parts 1 and 2 and 3, they total 6, which is exactly equal to the original number [6] with no remainder or minus. You should know that among [the] single digit [numbers], no other number remains integral in its parts except 6. In the tens [double digits] there is 28, in the hundreds [triple digits] there is 196, in the thousands [quadruple digits] there is 8,124, and so on.

"You should also know that the number 6 includes the shapes... [of everything] in the realm of physical existence.... [There are] three shapes, which are circular, square and triangular.... It is already known that the shape of a triangle, before the lines are drawn, is indicated by 3 points, and a square is indicated by 4 points. Therefore you should know that a circle is indicated by 6 points, for when you make a circle with a compass and measure out on the circle all around, along the whole course of the compass's leg, marking [equal distances] with dots, there will be a total of 6 dots. When an [equidistant] line is then drawn from each dot to the next, the measure of each line between two dots is the same as the measure of half the circle's diameter [i.e., the radius], and there will be 6 lines, like the number of dots, etc."

Index